COACHING DYNAMICS

EFFECTIVE COACHING AND MANAGEMENT OF TOP LEVEL TEAMS

BY
MATT DRIVER
AND
STEVE NICOL

**Library of Congress
Cataloging - in - Publication Data**

Coaching Dynamics
Effective Coaching and Management
of Top Level Teams
Matt Driver and Steve Nicol
ISBN No. 1-59164-070-9
Lib. of Congress Catalog No. 2003098072
© 2003

*Art Direction, Diagrams,
Layout and Editing*
Bryan R. Beaver

Cover Photo by
Jerry Coli

Printed by
DATA REPRODUCTIONS
Auburn, Michigan

Reedswain Publishing
612 Pughtown Road
Spring City, PA 19475
800.331.5191
www.reedswain.com
info@reedswain.com

TABLE OF CONTENTS

INTRODUCTION

Recently I was running around our training ground with our Head Coach, Steve Nicol, and our squad. It was early in the morning and it was a cold, damp New England day. The air was fresh and as the rain increased to a very steady downpour, even though I was wearing the appropriate warm-ups and rain gear, I was absolutely drenched. As we slow down to begin our stretching routine with the players, I turned to Steve and said "If I don't thank you every day, give me a slap." Simply put, I love my job.

We are few, but very fortunate to be in a profession that we not only have a passion for, but provides us with a different challenge on a daily basis. You see, it is not just about the X's and O's, if only it was that simple. Cookie (Malcolm Cook) explains it best when he said "Soccer coaching and team management is a multi-faceted occupation. It involves the effective communication of technical knowledge, important decision making and the delicate handling of many different types of personalities, as well as the ability to demonstrate in practice a high standard of soccer."

It is my belief that to be a coach, you need to be a visionary. A visionary that has the ability to convey his vision effectively, that will enable the team to become a cohesive unit, to believe in themselves, to believe in their teammates, and have belief in you, the coach. It is you who has the task of guiding them in their search to not only be the best they can be as individuals but to maximize their potential within the team concept.

Becoming a coach isn't only about attending courses, reading books and studying hours of instructional videotapes. They all play their part in the process of self-education and help build experience. However, you must fully understand that the coach, as a powerful life force, a dynamic presence and personality, must be appropriate at all times. Some of the most successful coaches have not only possessed this dynamic life force, as well as an extremely good understanding and knowledge of the game, but have also possessed an uncanny knowledge of human nature. Coaches such as Rinus Michels, the Dutch visionary, who is responsible for the "Total Soccer Concept". Also, Bill

Shankly, the legendary Team Manager of Liverpool Football Club, who created, arguably, the greatest Liverpool dynasty of the 70's. More recently, Sir Alex Ferguson, Manchester United's guru, who fashioned a club languishing in the lower half of the English First Division into one of the greatest clubs in the world through, at that time, a totally unique program - their own Youth Policy.

It is my hope and that of my fellow collaborators, Steve Nicol, Chris Ramsey and Renato Cappabianco that the information contained within **Coaching Dynamics** works for you the way that it has worked for us. It is a straightforward approach to managing your players and also continuously challenging them within a training environment. Through this book, we have brought to you a multitude of training activities covering generic sessions such as pressing, possession, transition, speed of play, playing out of the back, playing out of midfield, and playing in the final third. The trick is to take these activities, adapt them to suit your requirements and make them your own.

Good luck to you, your team and the players you work with.

Matt Driver

FOREWORD

It has occurred to me many times during my own involvement in the sport that soccer is a unique participant activity-in every aspect of the game. The very essence of the game requires that all involved-even those involved as spectators-be active partici- pants rather than mere spectators. This is especially the case for coaching.

Coaching Dynamics, as the title indicates, is about a dynamic process-that of coaching soccer players in an active and energiz- ing way. It outlines a methodology that will keep players interest- ed in the context of a learning environment, while keeping the all important "fun factor" central to the approach. It is this approach that will keep players, especially young players, coming back for more. And it is this approach that will ultimately help instill atti- tudes that are necessary to build winning teams.

I have known three of the contributors for a number of years- either as a long standing colleague (in the case of Renato Capobianco), as a participating spectator of the Liverpool FC (in the case of Steve Nicol) and through Major League Soccer (in the case of Matt Driver). And of course, I have had an opportuni- ty to work with all three in their respective roles with the New England Revolution. All bring a unique background to the effort of writing a book about coaching. Their effort, presented here, is richer because of the diverse experiences they are able to share. Your coaching will be richer by sharing these experiences with them.

Sunil Gulati
Managing Director
Kraft Soccer Properties

MATT DRIVER'S ACKNOWLEDGEMENTS

It is with great appreciation and gratitude that I thank the many who have guided me on my never ending search to quench my desire for knowledge and personal growth within this incredible sport.

Steve Nicol
Steve Gorrie
Bob Bussiere
Dr. Lew Atkinson
Eddie Tremble
Malcolm Cook

And of course to my lovely wife, Karen, my mum, Margaret and my dad, Malcolm.

CONTRIBUTING COACHES

Steve Nicol
Chris Ramsey
Renato Capobianco

All who are exceptional individuals, whom I could not have done this without.

ABOUT THE AUTHORS

Matt Driver

Originally hired to join Steve Nicol's Revolution coaching staff as an interim assistant coach on June 6, 2002, Driver was elevated to assistant coach exactly five months later, securing his role with the team that he helped lead to MLS Cup 2002.

Driver had entered his sixth season as head coach of the South Jersey Barons (USL Pro Select League) in 2002 before coming to Foxboro. The Glasgow, Scotland native, who also served as technical director and chief operating officer for the Barons, holds a USSF "A" License, as well as an NSCAA Premier License and an NSCAA Advanced National Diploma. In addition, he carries a Brazilian "A" License and the Scottish Football Association "A" Introductory License. He was also the State Director of Coaching for the NSCAA and the Director of the Olympic Development Program for the state of Delaware.

As head coach of the Barons, Driver led the team to two regular season conference titles, one regular season national title and one appearance in the National Finals. Off the field, his leadership helped to elevate the South Jersey Barons into one of the most successful professional organizations in the United Soccer Leagues.

During his professional playing career, which began at the age of 17, Driver, a striker, played in three countries. In England he played with the Bury Football Club, formerly of the English third division, and Burnley Football Club, formerly of the English fourth division. Driver also enjoyed a stint with S.C. Herford, formerly of the second division of the German Bundesliga. He has also played in the United States with the Albany Capitals and the Boston Bolts of the American Soccer League.

Driver now resides in Marlborough with his wife, Karen.

Steve Nicol

Steve Nicol, one of the greatest players in Liverpool soccer history and the 2002 MLS Coach of the Year, enters his first full season as head coach of the New England Revolution. He signed a contract extension with the organization on November 6, 2002, which keeps him at the helm for the next two years.

Hired by the Revs as an assistant coach on January 10, 2002, Nicol took on the team's head coaching duties in an interim capacity on May 23, upon the dismissal of Fernando Clavijo. Nicol orchestrated a remarkable turnaround over the final two months of the season, including a pivotal 5-0-1 stretch to conclude the regular season. He was able to find the right mix of players for a team that had a tumultuous start, adding mid-season acquisitions Daouda Kante and Winston Griffiths into the lineup and watching first-year striker Taylor Twellman emerge as the league's leading scorer. He guided the franchise to its first Eastern Conference Championship and first MLS Cup appearance at Gillette Stadium on October 20.

Nicol, 41, has become a prominent figure in the New England soccer community since moving to Massachusetts in 1999. He began that year as a player/assistant coach for the Boston Bulldogs (then of the USL A-League) and moved into a head coaching role for the team on July 13, 1999. Nicol's first stint with the Revolution also came in 1999, as he was named interim head coach of the team in September, replacing Walter Zenga and winning both games he coached to close out that season. Nicol returned to the Bulldogs for the 2000 and 2001 seasons as player/coach before re-joining the Rev's staff at the start of the 2002 campaign.

Nicol, who was born in Irvine, Scotland, was 18 years old when his professional career began with Ayr Utd in Scotland. He went on to make 467 appearances for English powerhouse Liverpool between 1981 and 1995, during which time Liverpool was one of the world's top club teams. He was voted English Player of the Year in 1989. Nicol anchored the Liverpool defense that won four English League Titles, three English F.A. Cup Titles, and reached two European Championship Finals. In 1984, the team defeated Italian club Roma to capture the 1984 European Cup. Nicol made 27 appearances for the Scottish National Team, and started for Scotland in the 1986 World Cup in Mexico. He made his last appearance for the Scottish national side in 1992. He also played with Sheffield Wednesday and with Doncaster Rovers in England. He served as player/coach for First Division club Notts County in England in 1995.

Nicol resides in Hopkinton, MA, with his wife, Eleanor, his son, Michael, and his daughter, Katy.

PART 1
TEAM MANAGEMENT

VISIONING

Creating a vision for the team

"The key ingredient of a vision seen is a vision shared"

The vision should provide a clear and concise answer to "Why are we here?". The vision should also be a collective collaboration between all who are involved or will be impacted by the vision. This will enable you to determine your vision statement, providing you with structure and goals. This will also give you and the team the ability to measure your progress and motivate individuals by giving them ownership in the group and by empowering them.

Developing a vision statement (12 step program)

1.   Invite input from everyone involved with the team.
2.   Explain why they are there.
3.   Ask, "What are our strengths?".
4.   Ask, "What areas do we need to improve upon?".
5.   Ask, "How do we achieve this?".
6.   Ask, " What can you do as an individual that can aid in this process?".
7.   Ask "What makes this team unique or special?".
8.   Ask, "What our goals should be?".
9.   Break these down to the lowest common denominator.
10. Let the ideas and suggestions sink in.
11. Write a draft vision statement and discuss it with the team.
12. Make any changes that are necessary and then write the final vision statement.

EFFECTIVE COMMUNICATION

The difference between a manager and a coach is that a manager is mostly interested in the results and the coach is mostly interested in the process. With this in mind, one of the most important tools you will need to develop is good communication skills. In today's game we need to have the ability to explain, in various ways, for all the players to understand.

- Communication is a dynamic process when used correctly.

- To communicate effectively, one must listen effectively.

- Communication is circular, not linear.

By communicating to the players and addressing the team you are forming, effectively, a bond/trust between you and the players. By doing this you disarm the gossipmongers that every team has. Use face to face communication whenever possible, even when the news may not be pleasant. Be candid and have concern. This shows that you have respect for them, but be prepared. Conflict and confrontation are natural, but provide stimuli that are needed for creative and effective problem solving.

12 STEPS TO EFFECTIVE COMMUNICATION

1. Present the reason behind a decision prior to announcing it.
2. When delivering bad news to a player be honest and candid, but show concern (empathy).
3. Have an open door policy, be approachable.
4. Take an interest in the players' habits off the field as well as on it. This builds trust and keeps the lines of communication open.
5. A good communicator builds approachability by being honest, sharing information when appropriate, and by admitting when he makes mistakes.
6. Every time you communicate with someone it can go two ways. It can either strengthen or weaken your relationship.

7. At times a player may hear you, but not listen to you. Learn to identify this by reading their body language/signals. If this is the case, ask them if it makes sense at this time. After they respond with either yes or no, then reply why, and listen to their feedback.

8. When sensing that a player may be frustrated, give him the opportunity to vent that frustration with you behind closed doors, not in public.

9. When a player asks to speak to you, never refuse him. However, you decide the time and place and find out what the topic of the meeting is. This will give you time to prepare.

10. Always lay down your rules of engagement early. Players will respond positively to this. They want to know what is expected of them and why.

11. Don't give mixed signals. Your body language may say one thing and your words another. Get them in sync.

12. Communication can build barriers but also break them down. Communication is at its most powerful when your actions follow your words.

A Player's Perspective
Brian Kamler

If there is one thing that can set a player's mind at ease, it is effective communication from the coach. Everything on the field becomes a little easier when you know what is exactly expected of you on and off the field as a player and as part of the team.

Probably the number one thing a player wants from communication with his or her coach is honesty. We want to know where we stand on the team. Does the coach view me as a starter or reserve? All players wonder about this. The other thing that we want to know is how we are doing. On the field, am I playing well? Am I doing what is expected of me? Honest answers to these two questions are what every player is looking for. All we want is the honesty of thecoach. We may not always like what he has to say, but I can tell you I would much rather know where I stand than be guessing. It is no different than someone wanting to know where they stand at a regular job. If you are in a nine to five job, maybe you want to know how you can get promoted, if you fit into the company's plans or if there is any room to grow in your career. It is no different for soccer players, whether you play club ball at the U-16 level, college or the pros. Honesty is the best way to communicate with your players. I have been traded four times in my career and there were a couple times when the trades did not go down as smoothly as one would hope. The main reason for the rocky trades was because of bad communication and dishonesty. Effective communication is also how you explain how you want your team to play. The clearer it is to the player how the coach wants to play, hopefully the fewer the mistakes on the field. I had a coach in high school who was one of the best coaches I ever had. He told us he didn't mind physical errors, but he didn't want any mental errors. To do this, he communicated in practice exactly what was expected in certain situations. Soccer is a little different from other sports:

things are constantly changing on the field and players have to think on their own. But if they know what the coach wants in similar situations as a result of effective communication, mistakes will be kept to a minimum.

Lastly, have an open door policy. Having this policy gives a player a chance to talk with the coach about anything on the on or off the field. To be able to discuss problems or things they need help with in a one on one situation may bring more out about a player than just the on-field relationship. In the end, by presenting clear and precise communication about what is expected, hopefully we perform above and beyond expectations.

Brian Kamler challenging for a ball.

TEAM BUILDING

In most circumstances, team building only takes place when there is a decline in the team's performance and significant problems arise between the players. This obviously results in an acrimonious atmosphere, which creates low morale and a negative performance environment.

To understand how to recreate a positive environment, it is very unlikely that you will mend all the fences and problems between the players immediately. The only way that you will be able to move forward is to get to the bottom of what the real issues are. Before you can begin to rebuild the team morale, some of the issues that could possibly crop up are:

- A player has been dropped and has a following within the team.
- Poor results and players are not taking responsibility for their actions.
- Lack of accountability with a player.
- Lack of leadership within the team.
- Conflict between players and coach, players and players, management and players.
- Decisions that have an impact on the players negatively.

Once you have identified what the underlying problem is you can begin to address the issue or issues with the players. Now let's assume you have a straight up problem, a conflict between two sets of players that needs to be resolved. You need to go into it knowing that not all players are going to like each other. The task here is to at least get them on the same page. It is a lot easier to get them to acknowledge what the other player brings to the table. When this is achieved you are well on your way to developing respect for each other and respect is a very strong emotion that can lead to harmony within the team.

One way to help create harmony within the team is to create a common enemy so that the team refocuses its negative energy outwards rather that internally. This will create a "them against us" mentality and will act as a mechanism to help bring the players back together.

None of this is possible if you do not possess the strength and courage to constantly deal with players and challenge them to maintain the appropriate work ethic and effort of what is expected of a professional player. As the coach you are always dealing with the emotional strain of not accepting the lower standard of performance and effort that players unconsciously put forth.

TEAM DISCIPLINE

When discussing team structure, a very important topic that always needs to be addressed is player discipline. Personally, I have always been of the opinion that most players want to follow a code of conduct, on and off the field. The reasoning for this is that even though all players are created different, they all need to be treated the same. When it comes to player discipline your only task as the coach should be to be consistent with your decision making policy and hold the player accountable for his actions. Remember, he is there because of what he did, not you, so you should never feel guilty.

The best method that I have found is to implement a dress and behavior code of conduct and give it to the players in handbook form when they join the team. At that moment you are telling the player that you have standards and that the club's expectations are there for all to see and understand. The handbook will have other general information inside: contact numbers of other players and key personnel within the organization, directions to pick-up places or training facilities located off-site, information on pre-game meals 48 hours leading up to a game, diet and nutrition information as well as hydration methods. There will also be a clearly defined list of fines and suspensions for any and all disciplinary issues. What is paramount for the coach is that he implements his rules to all players equally, regardless of the player's seniority within the team. Failure to do so will compromise his position and discipline within the club, leading to a possible breakdown of team chemistry.

MANAGING CONFLICT WITHIN THE TEAM

In most cases when you begin your role as a coach with a new team or if you want to change the way an established team plays, you are inevitably going to come up against some minor issues of resistance. Now, rather than going in with guns blazing and preaching "My way or the highway!", you have to acknowledge that the players will need time to adapt to your new approach and understand why some players resist change. You may challenge a player to perform a new task that he may not be comfortable with. That player is now being asked to perform outside his comfort zone, which may or may not have an impact on his physical and mental performance. This could have a dramatic effect on fear or loss of status within the team that could eventually lead to a loss of playing time, leading to concerns about their own image within the team. Here are several points that can be used to reference.

- Communicate their responsibility to themselves and the team.
- Find out what their perceived value to the team is.
- Make sure you can match personal agendas to the team goal.
- See how this change may affect their prestige or power within the team.
- Research their past history within the team with regards to conflict or resistance to change.
- Be familiar with players who have personal differences with you that can affect your decision to change.

In most cases, by communicating effectively with your team, the players will buy into the change. However, no matter how you present your case, there will inevitably be one or more players who resist. This resistance at some level is going to escalate into conflict and although conflict is good, as I have stated before, it provides stimulus that is needed for creative and effective problem solving. It can, if not effectively dealt with, become a cancer that spreads throughout the team, creating factions within the group, forming cliques and becoming a hotbed for hostility, leading to a breakdown of team chemistry.

Understanding the various personalities that typically manifest in a competitive environment is only half the battle. You also need to know your own strengths and weaknesses and the tools you possess to deal with these individuals. If you do not possess all the tools to do so, and few rarely do, partner with someone close to you to strengthen your weaknesses. This is called complementary partnering, working with each other's strengths and eliminating weaknesses.

A Player's Perspective
Leo Cullen

The topic of managing conflict within the team, while extremely important to success at the highest level, initiates the idea of avoiding the conflict altogether with preparation and experience in this area. Already in my short career I have seen as many coaching staffs fail this task as I have seen succeed. All of my successful examples are staffs that truly understood the concept of managing twenty personalities in an attempt to find a winning chemistry. And more often than not those staffs were not given that chemistry to begin with (otherwise the previous coach wouldn't have been replaced). Instead they managed the existing conflicts by: weeding out previous "cancers", keeping those that fit their plan, and adding others that would ultimately strengthen it. There are no secrets to success in the business of professional sports, there are only secrets that lead to failure.

So many times I have seen potential for success inside a locker room go unfulfilled because of a coach's inability to manage his personalities. Those personalities are only conflicts if you allow them to be, and the single most important weapon against that conflict is communication. In the end, professional players only want one thing from their coaches, to be treated like professionals. Players cannot help but respect a coach when he makes a decision for no other reason than doing what is best for the team, and then verbalizes it. The idea may not be met with unanimous agreement, but it will be respected. As a coach you are never obligated to share your every thought with the players, but in my experience the practice of voicing your decisions has always been the most successful. It has been the coaches with a weakness in this area whom I have seen fail.

In understanding the power of communication with regards to both managing and avoiding conflict, it is even more important to be entirely confident in your preparation as a coach. You cannot effectively communicate with any of your players if yo don't have a plan that you believe in. Create that plan, and then surround yourself with the right personnel for the job. It is not quite so black and white as that, but communicating with your players individually and collectively is an extremely effective method for conflict management. In doing this you won't eliminate all conflicts, but you will definitely minimize the situations that ultimately lead to a breakdown in the team's chemistry and consequently its success.

If I have learned one thing in my playing career with regards to a future in coaching, it is to not complicate everything. Each successful staff has taught me to create an environment where everyone knows the team goal and, more importantly, their own roles in achieving that goal.

THE GAME WITHIN (THE TEAM)

1. **The Fault Finder** - Always whining.
2. **Rumor Monger** - A tattletale.
3. **Antagonist** - Will cause trouble anytime, anywhere.
4. **Virtuist** - Everything has to be perfect.
5. **The Purist** - Plays by the rules.
6. **Quick Tempered** - Hot headed, fiery type.
7. **Exhibitionist** - I, me, myself, show off all the time.
8. **The Unbeliever** - Will never trust anyone but himself.
9. **Prankster/Trickster** - Always good for a laugh.
10. **Scapegoat** - Will sacrifice for the good of the team.
11. **The Processor** - Takes everything on board and thinks about it.

THE GAME WITHIN (THE COACH)

1. **Experience** (life, professional, skilled).
2. **Authority** (to pick, to drop, to release a player).
3. **Discipline** (team & individual "self").
4. **Self-reliance** (knowing ones strengths).
5. **Rapport** (with players, technical staff).
6. **Applied Psychology** (helping the players believe).
7. **Motivation** (intrinsic and external).
8. **Trust** (of players).
9. **Emotional Intelligence** (street smarts)
10. **Communication** (skills)
11. **Organizational** (skills)

EXTREME COACHING STYLES
(THE COACH AS THE CHAMELEON)

Each person has a personality that is a powerful life force, which is totally unique to them. This personality has been shaped and developed over the years by many external influences, such as, social surroundings, parents, friends, knowledge, personal experiences and also internal emotions. These create drive, vision, ambition, feelings (good & bad), what's right, what's wrong and likes and dislikes. As a coach, you have developed a unique style that is suited to your personality. This has also been influenced by many of the same factors that everyone else's personality has. However, you have taken those personal experiences, your knowledge, be it learned or acquired, influence from mentors, and I guess an idea or vision of what type of coach you would most like to be. That may have been true in the past but not now. Now you have more of an advantage to becoming the type of coach you wan to be. By studying and examining the many coaches who have traveled down this path before, you can begin to see specific patterns. Therefore, by identifying the extreme characteristics of a personality and by categorizing these, we can now benefit from seeing what the advantages and disadvantages are that exist in each of these.

THE DICTATOR: Autocratic style, "my way or the highway", who's only idea of teamwork is believing that as long as everyone does exactly their told, that's teamwork. Leaves no room for interpretation, believes in winning his way and losing your way.
Advantages: You know where you stand. His team will know what is expected of them. Everybody is going to be on the same page. He will give his players direction.
Disadvantages: Does not like independent thinkers. He can be very volatile and temperamental. Expects it to be his way or no way. Team can turn against him if the results don't go his way.

THE DEMOCRAT: Buddy coach. Has great concern for all his players, how they feel, what they want and what they like. Believes in taking care of the players and the players will take care of the results.
Advantages: All the players like him, a good guy to play for. He

will create a comfortable playing environment and will not pressure you to win.
Disadvantages: Team will probably lack discipline, and direction. He will probably put up with lazy players and under achievers. He will not demand the best from you.

THE MYSTIC: A visionary, work totally of motivating the players. Pays little concern to tactics. Likes players with individual skill and ability. He believes that if he has a group of highly talented payers, he will win.
Advantages: Loves players to take control. Likes to see creative players. Is probably a good man manager and will have brilliant ideas on how to play.
Disadvantages: Probably a poor organizer. Pays little concern to systems of play/tactics. The team probably lacks self-discipline and direction.

THE PLANNER: Analytical. Pays attention to the tiniest detail. Has a statistic for everything. He is tactically minded and likes to have his players very much like his ducks all in a row.
Advantages: His teams are always well organized and have structure. All are well informed about the opposition. Leaves no stone unturned. Wants team to play to the plan. Answers all questions.
Disadvantages: His team is less likely to be creative. Players won't to be able to solve problems on their own. The team will be very predictable and not be allowed to sway from his plan.

THE WHEELER DEALER: Shifty in nature. A smooth talker that will convince all those around him that they can do anything. He will always be looking out for the next best thing and will always be looking for an edge. He operates on the fringe.
Advantages: His team will always have good players. He will most probably be a good motivator. Will always give you the positive version. Will tell you what you want to hear.
Disadvantages: Nothing is entirely how it seems. He will tell the players what they need to know. His players will never get a straight answer and will push the boundaries on and off the field. You will never know where you truly stand.

POLITICAL STRATEGIST: Mushroom style of coaching. Believes in keeping everyone in the dark. Will only tell you what he believes you need to know. Likes to use this technique to keep players on their toes by keeping them on the edge.
Advantages: Never confrontational with his players. Players only have to do what is expected.
Disadvantages: Never gets close to his players. He keeps his players uninformed. Will not cultivate team spirit. Players don't play for him through belief, they play, for play. Cultivates a cold climate approach to playing. His door is always closed. He is probably a poor communicator.

By example, these are just a few of the extreme characteristics that can be categorized by these coaching styles. However, it seems clear to me that as a coach you are expected to deal with the many types of personalities that simmer in that melting pot we call a team. You, the coach, you, the manager, you, the psychologist, and you, the friend, need to be chameleon-like in nature and be able to adapt your own individual coaching style to the personalities and the situations that can arise. If you do not have this ability, acquire it, learn it, get it fast, as failure to do so will result in you, the coach, failing. If you only have fixed style of coaching or management, you will have a short-lived career. Even if you do manage to be successful in the beginning, it will be short lived.

For example, let's assume that you have The Mystic style of coaching and you have acquired a fantastic group of players that are motivated and believe in you, but are just not getting it right on game day. Let's say you have managed to identify that they are tactically weak and unorganized. It is at this stage you need to become more of The Organizer and get your players back on track by organizing them tactically and giving the players the information they need, that will enable them to be successful by playing in a framework. The other way is to have an assistant that compliments your style by bringing his strengths to complement your weaknesses. Therefore, between the two of you, you have it covered. This is called complementary partnering.

PART 2
PLAYER DYNAMICS

PLAYER MANAGEMENT

Player management has never been an easy subject. Even some of the best tacticians in the game have failed because of their lack of social and communication skills. There is no one perfect way of managing players. Different coaches have tackled this issue in different ways. A rule that has worked well for me quite simply is "if it's important to the player, make it important to you". This may sound a bit cliché but you should always give the player the benefit of the doubt until you are absolutely otherwise. When relationships break down between the players and the coach it can be due to a number of reasons: mistrust between the players and the coach, communication has broken down, the player may feel alienated from the rest of the team, etc. In any case, the one thing a coach should never do is attack the player personally. When this occurs, the player closes down immediately. Players can, and will, accept a coach critiquing and even attacking their performance as long as the coach has been consistent in his comments with the other players.

Depending on the level you coach you don't need to meet with a player all the time. However, you should have an open door policy so that if a player feels it necessary to meet with you, he knows you are available to discuss his issues. I have always operated under this scenario, as long as the player informs me of the subject matter beforehand so I am at least prepared for the meeting. On the flip side, I do not always feel it necessary to meet in my office, not unless it is for disciplinary matters. In that case then I would always have a member of my coaching staff in attendance so there is never any questionable issues that may arise at a later date after the meeting. A good way to meet with a player is to talk to the player after practice as you both are leaving the training field. It is a less threatening environment for the player and you can discuss most topics in this environment. The two aspects of player management that most coaches loathe are dropping a player or leaving players out of the line-up. Taking the player to one side at a convenient time is the most appropriate way of performing this unpleasant task. By doing it this way you are showing respect for the players and professionalism.

PLAYER ACCOUNTABILITY

When it comes to player discipline, creating a code of conduct is a relatively easy task. However, it becomes a pointless exercise when the standards you set are broken and you are not prepared to follow through with the consequences. I honestly believe that all players want discipline. Some may not know they want it, and those who know they want it, admit they need it. However, all players want to know what the parameters are. There is one thing for sure, at some time you will be called out and challenged, so be prepared to follow through and implement the appropriate punishment.

There are three basic rules to follow if you are to implement a code of conduct.

1. Rules need to be clear, concise and not open to interpretation.
2. Be impartial and consistent with everyone (no exceptions).
3. Always remember that the reason the players need discipline is that they were the ones who broke the rules, not you.

PLAYER FAMILIARITY

Regardless of what level you coach, all coaches need to know as much information about the player off the field as on it. Being familiar with a player's personal traits or technical nuances can definitely have its advantages. You've heard the saying "knowledge is power". I believe it's how you use your knowledge that gives you the power. In reality you are not always going to know exactly what your players are thinking but you can definitely get a feel for how they generally think and act. However, you must always be aware and communicate with them. You should use your staff to aid you in this process so you can build as complete a picture as possible. You can begin with a simple player profile template to assist you.

Technical	- Skills required for specific position.
Tactical	- Understanding and awareness of their role.
Physical	- Position specific strengths.
Psychological	- Motivating factors, internal, external, intrinsic.
Attitude	- Accepts role in a professional manner.
Chemistry	- Works well with others/doesn't work well with others
Personality	- Exhibitionist, private, jovial, antagonist, etc.

You can imagine how powerful a tool this can be if used effectively as a coach. However, you can imagine how powerful this could be if your players bought into applying this method to each other, helping them understand what makes one another tick in a positive way off the field as well as on it.

Players have a need to identify each other's individual nuances on the field. This can lead to easier communication and direction through audible and visual cues. It may also minimize confrontation but not to the extent of challenging each other on a professional level.

EMOTIONAL INVESTMENT

At some time a coach may find that he has several players within his team who have their own personal agendas, regardless of their playing ability. If and when this occurs, and cannot be brought under control, it will almost certainly lead to poor team chemistry and below par performance.

What is needed to avoid any such issues is to get your players emotionally invested in the team. By inviting your players to collaborate with you on some of the planning and preparation of the team's goals and objectives for the up coming season, you create an atmosphere of shared goals and responsibilities. Some of the areas that could be discussed could include the tactical direction of the team, system of play, formation, and the reason why. Set plays allow the players to experiment with their own ideas, utilizing their skills and abilities and of course team discipline, letting the players set the rules of conduct, holding each other accountable for their actions. By doing so you have empowered them in such a positive way that they now feel compelled to do the right thing. The players will feel there is value in everything that they do right, and what they do right as individuals will make a positive impact on the team.

A Player's Perspective
Jay Heaps

Team chemistry is essential for team success. Coaches must understand the importance of team chemistry and create an environment that enhances it. Having played at both the college and professional levels, I have seen the importance of the coach's ability to help a team come together. There have also been experiences when a coach has hurt the potential of a team by hindering the team's chemistry. At any level, players will sometimes put their own personal goals before the team's goals. I have seen coaches let this get out of control and it festers a negative attitude within the team. It becomes contagious and soon everyone is playing for themselves rather than the team. When this happens, players begin to blame each other and do not look within to correct the problems. In my experiences, some coaches let this go too far and it becomes impossible to turn the team around. However, I have also experienced situations where a coach has prevented such problems within the team. The coach creates an environment where the team is always first. Every player needs to know the team goals and strive to achieve them. When players work together toward a team goal, they think less and less about their own personal agendas. In turn, more awards and accolades go to individuals on successful teams.

As coaches include their players in what the team is doing, they must also be honest and forthright with each player. In my experience, honesty has been crucial for any team to come together and be successful. Players do not respect coaches who are not truthful about their role within the team. A player-coach relationship must be based upon honesty. That is not to say that a player's role will not change throughout a season, but it is important for the coach to speak candidly to the player about these role changes. For example, coaches often change the lineup and put players who are normally starters on the substitutes bench. These simple lineup changes happen all the time, but they can lead to chemistry problems if the coach does not approach it honestly and truthfully. On one occasion, a coach made the lineup change on game day without telling the player or the team before the lineup was posted. This situation became the players' focus, causing an unnecessary distraction and likely affecting the team's performance in the match. On the positive end of the spectrum, I have experienced a change in the lineup when the coach approached the player before the change was made and posted to the team. In the conversation, the coach made it clear why he was making the change. The reason why the change is being made is not up for discussion, but the player feels that the coach has a certain respect for him, and in turn continues to believe in the goals of the team.

Matt Driver, Jay Heaps and Leo Cullen before a match.

PART 3
TECHNICAL DEPARTMENT

DEVELOPING AN INFRASTRUCTURE (TECHNICAL STAFF)

On the appointment of a head coach there are many tasks that need to be implemented. Arguably one of the first is the selection of his technical staff. In most cases the head coach appoints an assistant, one that complements his weaknesses and partners his strengths. The buzzword for this is "complementary partnering". Every coach, or person in authority, looks for different qualities and has a different perspective on what they are looking for. The key, I believe, is finding what you believe your needs are in that person and then press on regardless. When compiling your technical staff you need to take into account your budget. This will depend drastically upon the level of your team and the resources at your disposal. One of the exercises I have always used, regardless of playing level, is to write down a wish list prioritizing my needs, in order. For instance:

Head Coach - Vision and plan.
Assistant Coach - Analyst and training sessions.
Goalkeeper Coach - Technical development.
Trainer - Pre and post care, treatment injuries.
Doctor - Orthopedic.
Team Administrator - Travel, league, meals, hotels, transport, etc.
Equipment Manager - Practice and game day duties.
Fitness Expert - General and position specific training.
Masseur - Player wellness program.
Chiropractor - Player wellness program.
Psychologist - Player wellness program.
Videographer - Needed to videotape games and practices.

Once you have gone through this exercise you can narrow your list down to what your exact needs are, depending on your budget. If you are in the minor leagues you can still compile a professional group by being creative through marketing concepts and trade deals.

After identifying your staff, you then need to organize a group meeting announcing your plan and vision and issue a clear understanding of what everyone's role is and what is expected of them. At this stage, depending upon what managerial style you have, you may want to have a brain-storming session to refine your plan and, more importantly, to get your staff emotionally invested into your program, making it equally important to them to share your vision.

DEVELOPING A TIMELINE/CALENDAR

January: (Last week of the month). Players will report to club, physicals are given and the beginning of pre-season begins. First week with strength and conditioning coach, selection of trialists, implement visioning and goals.

February: Pre-season continues in second week with strength and conditioning coach, selection of trialists to strengthen squad, recommendations from scouts, video tapes, agents, personal contacts. In February we go to training camp in a warmer weather climate to bed in basic technical, tactical and physical elements for two weeks.

March: Continue with pre-season. Now that we are in some kind of basic shape, we play against varied opposition. We should still be looking at key players who can strengthen the squad, but now we are looking to become faster, stronger and smarter. We will be playing more competitive matches with the emphasis on tactical shape and game fitness. At the end of March, the last week or so, we will again look to take players away for a 10-14 day training camp.

April: Competitive training situations are now key, as key players will have been selected to begin the season in specific roles. The players will be 85-90% at their physical peak so the emphasis in practice will be tactical and psychological. This is a time when your player management skills come into play. Players become nervous and antsy as the season is about to begin.

Mid-late April: The season begins. Your squad should be organized in its tactical shape. The team should be ready physically, and enthusiastic about the first game of the season.

May: The results and the way the team is performing will determine your next move. The key, however, is to know how many games you are playing that month. Normally, games will be on Saturday, so when you get into the daily grind of training every day and preparing for matches, you need to keep in mind that you have to keep the players fresh and enthusiastic for the up coming games.

June: Let's presume that the team is not performing as expected. Players that are key to results are injured or not emotionally getting on with each other. You will have decisions to make on how to deal with this. How you move forward at this juncture will be key to how your season will continue. Don't assume anything. Prepare for the best, but expect the worst.

July: Players that have been injured are back. You have managed to implement a sense of team chemistry with your rogue players, through whatever methods you have used, and the results are turning the corner. For you, things look good. Your new task is now trying to keep it running smoothly and also to keep the players fresh. Again, you should plan your practices around keeping the players mentally fit as well as physically sharp. Short intense practices are the way to do this, no longer that 1 ¼ to 1 ½ hours. The tactical side should be well bedded in by now and each player's role should be very clear.

August: Same as July, pretty much keep the personalities going in the right direction and occasionally, if needed, have individual and team meetings to reinforce the team's vision. The team should now be in a good position to make a push for a place in the play-offs.

September: Players can become emotionally drained. Giving them time off is good if they need it, but a day out as a team instead of practice is a good way also for getting a rest. It is key to remember that they have been going eight months now and they need to be stimulated a different way. However, be focused on each game as it comes.

October: Play-offs. A player's attention should only be focussed on each game as it comes. Appropriate amounts of rest and work is essential for a good run at the play-offs. When the player is not preparing for the game, he should be well relaxed mentally and physically, and once again balance, guidance and experience is what is needed to be successful in any tournament. As a coach it is up to you to provide them with this.

November: Regardless of your success in the season, you need to sit down and report on your team's exploits over the year. A good source of reference would be to keep a diary on individual player performances and team results and of daily happenings on the practice field. It is on this information that your selection of personnel for the up coming season will be based and also the facts that may be required to release a player who has struggled for whatever reason to ground himself into the team. At this time you will also have your exit physicals and begin to reintroduce yourself to the research process to find specific players to strengthen your squad. You will also have an exit meeting with the team and individuals, if needed, depending on the situation. After the meeting you will give the players the start date of pre-season, if you are giving them off until January. You may bring the players in for a mini camp after 6 weeks to monitor fitness. Time off isn't lazy time, it should be for active rest.

December: Travel, videos, agents, players. You will have to scout from as many sources as you can to find what you are looking for. You will attend tryouts, youth and college competitions, minor league games, etc. You must try to narrow it down to 5-6 players for your squad for next season. You will also be working closely with your staff to define roles and tasks that need to be addressed and also plan your pre-season schedule of training and games.

January: Redefine the process and repeat. Good luck.

2003 PRE-SEASON OBJECTIVES

Going into pre-season we have identified areas that we believe are our strengths and areas of concern that need to be addressed at this time. These areas will be broken down into individual sections and addressed over the course of the pre-season.

STRENGTHS	AREAS OF CONCERN
Team Shape	Possession
Team Defending	Transitional Play
Attacking Wide Right	Lack of Flair
Organization	Team Passing
Good Chemistry	1 or 2 Egos
Good Discipline	Lack of Team Speed
Individual Resolve	Set Plays - Free Kicks and Corners
Individual Player Sacrifice	Long Distance Shooting
Leadership	Speed of Play
Shooting	
Team Personality	
Confidence	
Consistency	
Set Plays - Defensive and throwins	

PRESEASON TRAINING PROGRAM

PLAYER PROFILE
Areas that should be considered, but not limited to:

- Body Fat - Measured by the percentage of fat.
- Endurance - Measured by the beep test.
- Recovery - Measured by yo-yo test
- Quickness - Measured by the 40 yard dash

Along with those tests there should be a general strength and conditioning program, progressing to position specific, as well as various tests to monitor progress.

Week One: Base testing and general strength and conditioning program designed in conjunction with our coaching staff, fitness coach and physio.

Week Two: A continuation of the strength and conditioning program with testing at the end of the two week initiation.

BRAZIL

Week Three: A reintroduction to the ball, objective here is to maximize the players' touches on the ball, developing technique and endurance. This will be accomplished through a series of exercises that will be challenging, competitive and enjoyable. Two sessions a day, 10:00 a.m. - 12:00 noon and 4:00 p.m. - 6:00 p.m.

Week Four: The beginning of our foundation work. We begin by introducing the players to our philosophy and methodology by implementing individual and small group tactics. Topics such as defending, pressing, possession and transitional play. Return home.

Rest Period: Five days off on the return to the United States.

NEW ENGLAND

Location dependent upon the weather. Most likely indoors in the bubble.

Week Five: A series of small sided, transitional activities will be designed to maintain our level of endurance and enhance our quickness by implementing a speed and perception program. This, however, must be monitored and the appropriate rest period has to be followed to maximize results. For example:

Monday	10:00 a.m. - 12:00 noon Speed & Perception 4:00 p.m. - 6:00 p.m. Gym
Tuesday	Off
Wednesday	10:00 a.m. - 12:00 noon Speed & Perception 4:00 p.m. - 6:00 p.m. Gym
Thursday	Off
Friday	10:00 a.m. - 12:00 noon Speed & Perception 4:00 p.m. - 6:00 p.m. Gym
Saturday	a.m. - 11 v 11

Week Six: A repeat of week five with slight modification. We could include training with heart monitors to maximize work rate and also administer some individual and team testing to monitor progress.

Rest Period: Number of days to be determined.

COSTA RICA

Week Seven: Morning Sessions - Develop team shape and balance, in small groups (4v4, 6v6, 8v8), in activities such as blocks, pressing and transitional play. Afternoon Sessions - Team tactics. Playing in a couple of formations such as 3-5-2, 4-4-2 and 4-5-1. Identify strengths and weaknesses as well as implementing as a team our individual and small group tactics with explanation of triggers and visual cues (when, where and why).

Week Eight: Morning Sessions - Transitional play in large
groups. These activities will encompass a large
variety of tactics and challenges that will create
competitiveness and develop a consistent rhythm
of play.
Afternoon Sessions - We will play full sided games
and look to refine our team tactics in a whole-part-
whole scenario. For example, if the strikers'
movement is not in tandem we will, at the time,
address it within the team concept. Return home.

Rest Period: To be determined.

Weeks Nine, Ten & Eleven:
Play, play and play. Our objective in the final weeks prior to the
start of our season would be to identify our strengths and refine
them. Also, we would like to address any areas of concern,
streamline our system of play, organize our set plays for and
against, and keep the tempo of our sessions high spirited, competitive and enjoyable. Over the course of the pre-season, develop a team chemistry that will maintain our level of expectations
within the team.

TECHNICAL (SCOUTING) DEPARTMENT REPORT

Video Analysis

In today's game, using every possible method of analysis in
scouting your opponent can give you an added advantage.
However, video has many other uses.

Scouting Report
When used in conjunction with a scouting report, video can
address specific areas that a coach would want to highlight on
the opposition. For example, individual players, set plays, formation, system of play, strengths and weaknesses of the team.

Team Talk
Video is good to use when addressing matters of concern within
your own team and individual performances. However, it is good

to remember not just to point out the negative situations on tape but also the positive ones, as a visual guide is far more powerful than a verbal reference, which after all, to a player, is only an opinion.

Individual Benefits
Many players have been known to use video as a way of improving their own performance, from technical to tactical implications.

Motivation and Video
Several teams have been known to use video to motivate their players. One such way is to put a highlight tape together of several players achieving or accomplishing tasks or goals, partnered with some inspirational music. This can be shown to the players the day before a big game to make an impact on them and have an effect on the outcome.

SCOUTING (TECHNICAL) REPORT

Weather conditions: _____   Opposition: _____

Field condition: _____   Date of game: _____

Time of kick off: _____

Team Shape _____   **Starting line up** _____

_____   Goalkeeper - _____

System of Play _____   Defender - _____

_____   Defender - _____

_____   Defender - _____

_____   Midfielder - _____

_____   Midfielder - _____

_____   Midfielder - _____

_____   Midfielder - _____

_____   Midfielder - _____

_____   Forward - _____

_____   Forward - _____

_____

Free Kicks For _____   **Individual player nuances** _____

_____   1. _____

_____   2. _____

_____   3. _____

_____   4. _____

_____   5. _____

_____   6. _____

_____   7. _____

_____   8. _____

_____   9. _____

_____   10. _____

_____   11. _____

Free Kicks Against _____

_____

Corners For and Against _____   **Key Players** _____

_____   1. _____

_____   2. _____

_____   3. _____

_____   4. _____

_____   5. _____

Defensive Tendencies

- Set plays against
- Direct/indirect play
- Pattern of play
- Weak players

Attacking Tendencies

- Set plays for
- Direct/indirect play
- Patterns of play
- Strong/key players

Overall view and comments

- Look at strengths and weaknesses
- Match ups between your strengths and their weaknesses

ACTUAL REPORT PRIOR TO REVOLUTION 3-1 VICTORY OVER L.D. ALAJEELENA (COSTA RICA'S NATIONAL CHAMPIONS)

OVERVIEW

They definitely favor a South American/Brazilian style of play but don't really have the personnel to implement it fully. The back four give the ball away when pressured and still they consider trying to be clever. The midfield and strikers are very dynamic going forward, with quick transitional movements with and without the ball. When they go forward they throw everything at it without due care and attention to what could happen when their attack breaks down. What happens is that they leave huge holes between the attacking wave of players and defenders who stay and don't work as hard to get back as they do in going forward. They are an extremely physical team, cynical in their tackling on and of the ball, so do not switch off at any time. This game took place in front of 17,000 passionate fans that drove the team on to a resounding victory of 4-1 against a team that may have won the game early on if they had not blown their chances. The referee sent four people off in this game, 1 from Alajeelena, 2 from Suspria and the coach from Alajeelena. "Do not talk back". They are more likely to let bad tackling go than dissent.

What you can expect is a hot blooded, highly intense, fiercely competitive night and that is just from the fans. Beware of quick restarts and free kicks especially standing on the ball

INDIVIDUAL PLAYER TENDENCIES

Goalkeeper #1: Handling was poor. Parries a lot of shots. Terrible at setting up walls. Second week in a row that he has been beaten on the same side.

Right Fullback #8: Likes to go forward. Links well with #10. Very quick and wants to get involved in the attack as much as possible.

Left Fullback #12: Quick plays, small. Has poor distribution. Gets forward but not as much as #8.

Centerback #3: Big, strong, physical player. Dives in too much. Leaves foot in. Lacks pace. Bad on the ball. Very erratic. Poor decision-maker. (Captain)

Centerback #24: Big, strong, physical player. Will go through you when possible. Sweeps, very slow, does not distribute well. Good in the air.

Defensive Midi #5: Physical presence. Sits in front of the two centerbacks. A ball winner. Doesn't get forward much. Good in the challenge. Definitely the 5th defender. Distribution above average. Plays it short most of the time.

Attacking Midi #17: Plays as a third striker mostly. Makes a lot of penetrating runs, especially off #10 and #29. Arrives from behind. Hard to pick up. Good pace. Will run at you if he has the ball. Will not track back. Plays one way.

Right Midi #10: Great left foot, no right. Links up well with #8 and #29. Comes inside onto the left. Very good on the ball. Great passer. Sees things early. Dangerous. However, he left the game after 38 minutes with a thigh strain. #9 entered the game and was very effective.

Left Midi #13: Good player. Likes to run at players. Gets forward well. Has very good pace and is technically good. Moved back to cover when the team went down a man late in the second half.

Right Striker #29: Extremely dangerous. Very quick, technical player. Can play balls off or take you on. Can't let him turn. Not a big lad, but strong. Very fast and good in the air. Every time he had the ball he was a danger. Got subbed when they went to 10 men.

Left Striker #7: Good pace. Will shoot from any distance. Scored a screamer 35-40 yards out. Finishes well and supports well.

Unselfish. Set up a couple of goals by combining with the mid-field and other striker. Dangerous.

Subs #9 & #15: Did great when they came on in their respective roles. #9 was dangerous going forward. #15 defensively in mid was excellent for #5. Strong athletic players.

DEFENSIVE TENDENCIES

Back four were very erratic and made poor decisions when they were put under pressure. They still tried to play the ball out through the middle of the field and gave the ball away an awful lot. The two outside defenders alternate going forward, leaving three at the back. This happens when the midfield diamond has squeezed the space allowing the defender the room to make the run down the line. The two center defenders have no pace and lack technical ability. They will mug you if you hold on to it too long. #24 is good in the air and may come up for corners. #5 sits in front of the back four and cuts out a lot of balls, but when he is drawn out of position the two center backs, #3 and #24, struggle. Both these players lack mobility. We should try to run at them when the opportunity presents itself. If we play out of the back slowly and try to play through the middle, the two strikers will close you down, giving the rest of the team time to get behind the ball. They work hard to win the ball in their attacking third. If we play it quickly and a little more direct, with good use of the flanks, we can catch this lot out by using the space in wide areas, as they leave themselves wide open to a quick counter. At set plays they pack it in (defensively), but never have a player on the back post and the player on the near post stands a yard off it. They are very unorganized at free kicks (against). The goalkeeper has been beaten twice in two weeks after he set up his wall. On both occasions he was standing on the side he had set the wall up and both shots flew past him on that side. So they will be wary of this.

MIDFIELD TENDENCIES

Diamond in midfield, very similar to how the Brazilian teams play.
Both right and left side midi's squeeze play centrally. #5 & #17
have very specified roles. #5 sits in and supports and plays
almost 80-90% defensively allowing #17 to stay high all the time.
#17 likes to make his runs from behind the front two, making it
difficult for defenders to pick him up. Both right and left sided
midis squeeze, allowing the appropriate fullback to get forward.
They definitely favor the right side even when #10 left the field.
#8 made significantly more runs forward. The midfield unit is
very dangerous going forward, linking up well with the strikers.
The down side for them is that they leave themselves open to
counter attacks as they don't transition well in defensive situations. As soon as the ball turns over they are vulnerable. On
many occasions they seemed like two teams, 5-6 attacking, 4-5
defenders. Both subs that came on were in midfield. The first,
#9, came on for #10 who limped out of the game with a thigh
strain. #9 was effective, strong and mobile. #15 came on for
#29. This was later on in the game and immediately after they
had 9 men. #5 was sent off for a second yellow. Defensive midi
for a striker and moved their formation into a 3-4-2. Their style
changed to a counter attacking style through midfield. They actually took the lead at 1-1 to 2-1, 10 v 11, due to breaking runs
from midfield. #7 scored a screamer 35-40 yards out, bottom
corner.

ATTACKING TENDENCIES

The front two have very good pace and excellent work rate.
They begin the attack by pressing at the edge of their attacking
third. This is only effective if, like Suspria, we play it short and
tight out of the back. They begin their attack from the back and
favor forcing it through the middle of the park, playing it short and
getting numbers in that area, preferring only to go to the flanks
when they get into the attacking third. #29, a striker, has a good
all round ability and is very creative on the ball, can hold it up or
go at you. He is supported by #7 who creates space and opportunities for the #17, the attacking midi, to make his penetrating

runs from behind them, making it difficult for defenders to pick him up. Our goalkeeper needs to watch for this lad. Be ready to step in behind the defenders depending on how close the back four is to him. The front two, however, elect to do most of their work in the attacking half, so whenever they have been played out of the game they don't work all the way back. At set plays, free kicks outside the box and the shot is not on and corner kicks they always favor to go to the far post with decoy runs near and a player spinning out to go to the back. Some of the balls did not reach their intended targets but the runs were made.

PREPARING FOR GAME DAY (DAY BEFORE)

First phase of warm up: Progression to full 11 v 11, no restrictions game. 1 hour maximum. Warm up in team shape in an 11 v 11. The second 11 will play in the same tactical shape as the opposition. The ball will be played at low pace, no tackling or interceptions, just movement of balls in predetermined patterns to create visual cues for the players. This will also get the players mentally prepared. After 3-4 minutes, stop the players and have them stretch. As you repeat the process, you speed up the ball movement.

Second phase of warm up: The ball gets turned over to the opposition (second 11) and you are now moving at half pace. Your other objective at this stage is to take your defensive shape and sharpen up on your balance, rhythm and movement, as well as communication when the other team has the ball. Again you will halt the game and stretch. At this time you can make any adjustments to refine an individual or team movement.

Third phase of warm up: Both teams can play to match related conditions with a restriction of no tackling or interceptions. Teams work hard to keep the ball and move it quickly without fear of being tackled. This lasts for about 7-8 minutes. You then halt the game again. Have them stretch and make any adjustments or suggestions you deem necessary.

Final phase of warm up: Progress onto match conditions, full contact. Play for 15-20 minutes, implementing any and all set plays. Even if you must fabricate the situation to create a set play, this needs to get done. Only freeze or halt the game to get a coaching point in if it is really needed. If not, let them play.

DAY OF THE GAME

Pre-match meal
This should ideally be three hours before the game and consist of boiled or grilled chicken, pasta, vegetables (steamed), light broth or soup. No coffee, tea or soda. Plenty of water.

Players arrive
Players arrive 1½ hours before the game to be taped, walk the field, check conditions and equipment needed and change into warm up equipment.

Players' warm up
20-30 minutes. All players are different, but you should have a predetermined warm up that all players are comfortable with and that the coach or assistant coach can monitor just to be sure they are ready to begin when the whistle goes.

Players' team talk
10 minutes before they take the field the head coach will have his final words. He should have prepared them well enough that he needs only to hit specific bullet points of reference. For example, set plays and player responsibilities that may have been changed last minute. Most coaches will have the responsibilities of the set plays clearly marked on the wall with posters relating to each set play.

Players take the field
The game kicks off. You should have a note pad and pen to take notes on what you see, positive and negative. This will help you when you are giving your team talk at half time. Remember a player never makes mistakes, at least in his own mind. Give him facts, not opinions.

POST GAME TRAINING

What most coaches don't realize enough is the importance of the first day back to training after a game. What they do not seem to grasp is that this will, more than likely, be the trickiest session of the week, regardless of what went on physically during the previous game. Now, there are obviously going to be some things that you will have to accomplish in this session that will remain consistent throughout the season. You may have given the players a couple of days off to recover after the physical exertion of competition. You will have to make sure that on their return to the training ground, the players go through a real good warm up and stretching session, prior to progressing onto the more demanding, physical activities. This obviously aids in the recovery process, helping to flush out any remaining lactic acids which may lead to muscle soreness and stiffness. This is relatively easy to monitor, since it will be able to see how the players are moving and reacting to the training session. What is less obvious, and definitely what makes this session the trickiest, is to observe the psychological status of the individual players that make up the team and what is the overall general feeling of the team. This, in essence, may have been influenced by several factors, some of which may be, but not limited to:

1. Team results.
2. Overall team spirit.
3. Personal performances.
4. Player's private lives, etc., etc., etc.

The main topic that will influence a coach's approach to training is how the team played and the outcome of that game, what the result was. If you were unlucky enough to have a bad result and the team's overall performance was poor, the last thing, without question, that a coach would want to do in this day and age is to bring the players in to training and run them into the ground as a form of punishment. The problem with this is that you will more than likely turn the players against you and you will lose them. There is only one thing for certain that will definitely happen, you will need them to play for you at the end of the week (and that may be difficult). The key for me is to have a feel for you players. Regardless of the performance of the team, go about your duties in a professional, diligent manner. If you have had a disappointing result and you are definitely not happy with the situation, it is up to you on how you set the tone of the training session. You most definitely will have to lift the team morale, so your objective will be to lift the spirits of the players by implementing a high energy, high impact session. By doing so you will be getting the players to lower their guards and not to be defensive in their prepared response to the team's performance. Allowing you, the coach, to move on to prepare the team in a more positive environment.

If you team has had a favorable result and has performed in a positive way, you will still have to address various influencing factors, such as:

1. Inflated egos.
2. Lack of focus.
3. Relaxed approach to training.
4. Player's personal agendas, etc., etc., etc.

If team morale and spirits are too high players could be bordering on the verge of being overconfident. You, the coach, need to approach the team in a consistent, professional manner and knowing your players and having a feel for the team, sets the tone of the session by not over praising and reacting overconfident, but by diligently going about your duties in a consistent manner. Slowly bring the players back down to earth, but not diminishing their enthusiasm and appetite they have for the game.

All in all, if you are to get the best out of your players on a consistent basis, you yourself must be consistent, but also be able to manipulate the situation to suit your requirements. When you start will be when you get the players back on to the training ground. You should only glance back when moving forward.

DEVELOPING A TECHNICAL REPORT

On your appointment as coach you will have to evaluate as quickly as possible the current make up and political status of the team, without prejudice. To some extent it may be a huge advantage if you have inherited the team through promotion from within, since you will have an internal working relationship or previous knowledge of the players. However, if you are moving into a new club this can also be a positive situation as it gives you the ability to create a clean slate for the players, which may give some of them a reprieve from their individual situation. What you need to do is itemize each potential issue that might be a problem and address them systematically through a planned approach and determined team direction. For example, you may have inherited a team that has:

- Low team spirit.
- Lack of confidence (individual and team).
- Little tactical organization.
- Lack of accountability on and off the field.
- Poor player discipline.
- No communication between coaching staff and players.
- Player confrontations on and off the field.
- Inherited player issues.
- Mistrust of coaching staff.
- Undefined roles.

COACHES TECHNICAL REPORT

Potential/Pending Issues

There will almost certainly be a number of issues that will need to be resolved when you take over the reins at a new club. Some of these issues could be as follows:

- Player contracts.
- Team has just released the coach and players are feeling insecure about their position within the team.
- The team has lost a lot of games.
- Team chemistry is poor

- Player injuries are limiting team selection.
- Individual player issues.
- Tactical issues.

Almost all issues are solvable. You must, however, identify and report them, then prioritize them systematically and eliminate them one by one.

PLAYER EVALUATION

Player selection and availability is always an issue. After you have taken the time to assess the situation and you have determined the needs of the team, which will be predicted on your vision, you will need to make some tough decisions. You will now make an unbiased decision to retain or refrain. This has to be a totally unemotional decision and based entirely on the needs of the team.

Based on an 18-player squad, a suggested breakdown would be as follows:

Goalkeepers	Defenders	Midfielders	Strikers
GK 1	FB 1	Outside HB 1	Forward 1
GK 2	FB 2	Outside HB 2	Forward 2
	FB 3	Outside HB 3	Forward 3
	CB 4	Center Mid 4	Forward 4
	CB 5	Center Mid 5	
	CB 6	Center Mid 6	

Release - Player 1   **Team Needs**

Position: Rightback

Centerback

Big Forward

Trade - Players 2, 3, 4, 5 & 6   Fast Forward

Right Wing/Halfback

Questionable - Players 7 & 8

RECRUITMENT PROCESS

The recruitment process is vastly different at the various levels within soccer, whether it is youth or professional. Yet, regardless of the level, you must have a network of contacts, scouts, agents and other coaches. Enthusiasm is key. Many coaches let themselves down in this area and see it as the least exciting part of their profession. Successful coaches go about their business rather than hope the next best thing walks through the door.

1. Invite players in to tryout personally.
2. Video and references to be followed up on each player personally.
3. Personal contact is key and a first step to developing a potential relationship with the player.
4. Tryouts: keep them simple, let them play.
5. Look at the key components that make up the role you want that player to fulfill and use that as a potential starting point.
6. If you like a player and want that player ,tell him why you want him and what his role could be.
7. Finally, if you don't want a player, give him the respect and tell him personally.

TIMELINE

When preparing a technical report you need to add a timeline of actionable points. At the end of the day the powers that be will want to know if you have a plan that is structured and relevant to the task you have been given. You may also use the timeline as a motivating tool to keep your course, to get done what you set out to do.

For example:

October/November: Identify needs and clarify a budget with regards to player personnel. Develop a plan to secure personnel required.

*November/December:*Set tryout dates and secure venue for new recruits. Contact invited players, etc.

December/January: Players report for first part of pre-season. Strength and conditioning weeks one and two. Individual and small group tactics, etc.

January/February: Develop a system of play. Define player roles, etc.

February/March: Pre-season games. Determine set plays for and against. Experiment with player roles.

March/April: Finalize squad, tactics. Prepare to start the season in earnest. Win the first game of the season.

PART 4
PLAYER WELFARE

SOCCER FITNESS
by Renato Capobianco

When discussing fitness, the first thing that comes to mind is whether or not to incorporate the ball within your fitness session. Many studies have produced numbers that show that on average, a soccer player is in some form of possession of the ball for less than 5% of their time on the field. That would mean that 95% of the time they are moving around the field without the ball performing sprints, turns, jumps and tackles. This information leads me to believe that the majority of a team's fitness sessions should be conducted without the ball. Of course, one needs to take into consideration the age group and the number of training sessions per week when developing a fitness program. If you only have your team for two sessions per week, then your fitness sessions will make up less of your practice and you may want to incorporate the ball in order to make the best use of your time.

Soccer Specific Fitness

Is there such a thing as soccer specific fitness? The answer is yes. Soccer requires a solid aerobic base in conjunction with the ability to perform repeated intervals (i.e., sprints) in an anaerobic state. Simply put, an aerobic base will better allow you to recover from repeated intervals of anaerobic work. Ultimately, you want to be able to perform as many intervals of anaerobic work as possible before the intensity of each interval drops and/or you simply can't run anymore. In game terms, you want to be able to make those last three or four runs down the field in the last 5 minutes of the game when your opponent doesn't have anything left. This is when your anaerobic endurance takes over. And this is what the rest of this section will primarily deal with.

Anaerobic Endurance

I know this term sounds like an oxymoron. It's not. It simply means that a soccer player has to develop an ability to perform as many intervals of high intensity work as possible before his intensity significantly drops or he can't run anymore. Going on 4-5 mile runs isn't going to address this.

When designing a fitness session to improve anaerobic endurance, you should consider two different approaches. The first method involves having players do interval work through straight ahead running only. These sessions are good if you want to get a solid fitness session without overly taxing the leg muscles. An example of this type of session would be to have players run "box to box" sprints one length at a time (approximately 80 yards).

A second method of training anaerobic endurance is to incorporate acceleration/deceleration and change of direction in the running. A classic example of this form of training would be shuttle runs. While both methods will address anaerobic endurance, the latter will also develop the muscular endurance of the hip and leg muscles required to perform the constant changes of speed and direction that occur during a game. We have all seen instances where our players have reported to the first week of pre-season and boasted that they spent the off-season running 5 miles a day. They then proceed to keel over the first time they have to run up and down the field at full speed. They simply haven't trained for the type of running they're going to do in a game.

While both methods provide for good fitness sessions, the latter provides for more soccer specific fitness. It takes a tremendous amount of energy to accelerate, decelerate, and change directions. This type of fitness can also be very taxing on the lower limb muscles so you need to vary the type of fitness sessions you put your team through. Too many shuttle run sessions can wipe your team out. Keep the legs fresh by mixing it up. At the beginning of your season, take about two weeks to incorporate a high volume of shuttle work. Too much cutting and turning early on can lead to a rash of groin pulls. Once your season is in full swing, let the running done in games serve as your shuttle training and spend more of your fitness sessions on straight ahead running. By doing this, you'll save the players' legs for the all important games while still taxing the cardiovascular system.

When developing a fitness session that addresses anaerobic endurance, don't be afraid to mix up the distances and rest intervals. After all, during a soccer game players seldom if ever run the same distance over and over again. At the beginning of your season, I recommend a 4 to 1 work/rest ratio. As the season progresses you can eventually reduce this ratio to 2 to 1. It is also important to note that as a general rule, the shorter and more intense the interval of work, the more time you need to provide for a near complete recovery.

Pre Season 100 Yard Shuttles

A common mistake coaches make in pre-season is going all out during the first couple of fitness sessions. As much as we'd like to think that our players come in to pre-season ready

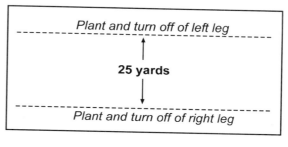

to go, in reality it is very different. Here is a 100 (4 X 25) yard shuttle that is to be run at no more that ¾ speed. The 100 yards is to be covered in 20 seconds with a 2 to 1 work/rest ratio. Most male soccer players over the age of 17 should be able to cover this distance in the 20 seconds allotted running at ¾ speed. Allow 24 seconds for females over the age 18 and 22 seconds for college or professional teams. Remind your players that the purpose of this shuttle is not to run it as fast as possible but to keep the turns as sharp as possible and come in at the determined time. Make sure that your players turn off of each leg equally. One way of ensuring this is to designate one end of the course as turning off the right leg and the other end off the left leg. With a 2 to 1 rest/work ratio, assign 3 players per line and make enough lines to accommodate the size of your team.

One last hint: Have players start each shuttle in something other than a straight ahead standing position. Vary between jogging in place, facing the course sideways or even with their backs to the course. Remember, you never know from what position you'll be asked to sprint from.

After performing this shuttle a few times, you can add a 5 yard "footwork zone" at one end of the course to further condition the abductors, adductors and glutes. When the players reach the far end of the course, they can either side shuffle, backpedal, or use a cross-over step over he first 5 yards before turning and accelerating the remaining 20 yards. Mark the 5 yard "footwork zone" with a cone. Emphasize a quick transition between the designated footwork and the ¾ sprint.

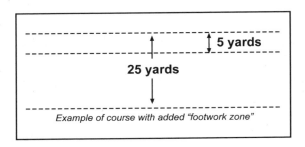

Example of course with added "footwork zone"

Fitness Testing

Let me take a moment to share with you my thoughts on fitness tests. For years, soccer coaches used variations of a two mile run to determine soccer fitness. This form of test also served to motivate players to train in the off-season. It wasn't uncommon for coaches to force players to run the test until they passed it. So for the majority of the off season, players would train to pass the fitness test, and not necessarily train to prepare themselves for the demands of a soccer game. Fortunately, most of the soccer coaching community has moved on from long distance testing and are now using some form of intermittent interval testing to determine their players' fitness levels.

My first criteria when choosing a fitness test is: What is it testing and how useful are the results? A fitness test should be able to give you information specific to the demands of a soccer game. Ideally, the test itself should also serve as a soccer specific fitness session and your players should be able to easily set up the test on their own. In this case, the 300-yard shuttle test requires only 25 yards and a stopwatch. The reason why I choose 25 yards instead of the standard 50 yard distance is because studies have shown that, on average, a soccer player will at most run 19-25 yards straight ahead before having to either change speed and directions, jump, or challenge for a ball.

The 300 yard shuttle run test has been used for many years in many different sports. The shuttle distance normally used is 50 yards, but it is not uncommon to see this test run over a 25 yard distance. The most commonly used method for using this test is having players cover the 300 yard distance as fast as possible, providing a 5 minute rest and then having them run the shuttle distance again and taking the average of the two times.

Administering the 300 Yard Shuttle Run

This particular 300 yard shuttle test should be administered as follows:

Players will run the shuttle test 4 times with 90 seconds rest between each trial. Unlike the standard 300 yard shuttle run where the players are asked to run as fast as possible, the purpose of this test is to have the players cover the distance under a specified time for all trials. If a player fails to complete any of the 4 shuttles under the specified time, he fails the test. You want to explain to your players that it is not to their benefit to run the first two trials as fast as possible if they can't meet the specified time for the third and fourth trials. Players should run the first three trials fast enough to meet the cut-off time and save their energy for the last trial.

This testing procedure will serve as a good field test for coaches to measure their team's recovery from interval work. The great thing about this test is that players can easily run this on their own during the off season and the test itself can serve as a useful fitness session at the end of small sided pick up game.

Here are some times (in seconds) that should be used as a guideline for different age groups:

Group	Male	Female
High School (Varsity)	66	72
College	63	66
Professional	61	64

Developing a Fitness Session

In order to take the guess work out of how much running should be included in a fitness session, I took a look at various soccer studies to determine how much running at ¾ to full speed is performed by a player during a professional soccer game. Most studies reported that a player would perform about 18% of his running at ¾ to full speed. Studies also tell us that on average, a player will cover between 6 and 8 miles during a game. So, if we take 18% of 7 miles, we can conclude that during a game a player covers approximately 2,200 yards at ¾ to full speed. With this number of 2,200 yards, we can now construct fitness sessions with a better idea of how much volume per session we should incorporate.

The next step in this process is to determine how much running you want to perform in a fitness session based on where you are in the season and/or what percentage of time the fitness session will take in the overall practice session. In order to quantify the progression of your fitness development, try the following method:

At the beginning of your season, your fitness sessions should be comprised of 60% (approx. 1330 yards) of the aforementioned 2,200 yards. Depending on the length of your pre-season, slowly progress so that by the first game, your fitness sessions are comprised of about 80% (1,800yards) of 2,200 yards. Again, depending on the length of your season, your fitness sessions should reach 2,200 yards somewhere between the third and fifth game. Remember that this volume of work is based on sessions that are comprised of intervals of short sprints (between 15 and 60 yards). If you divide, 1,800 yards by 30 (yards), you get 60 running intervals of work. being performed at ¾ to full speed. That's a lot of running! Add to that all the accelerating/decelerating and changes of direction and you have some very specific fitness sessions. You can see how this way of determining the progression of your fitness sessions can be beneficial towards planning for your season.

Fitness Session

Here are some interval fitness sessions that you can apply to the progression method described above. All the sessions address the following movement components:

- Acceleration/deceleration
- Change of direction
- Lateral footwork (for the conditioning of the abductors and adductors)
- Backpedaling

These components will work to condition the muscles involved in all the movements required during a game while the running itself will tax the cardiovascular system. Do not underestimate the importance of conditioning the body to perform specific muscles involved with changes of speed and direction. Once muscles fatigue, turns aren't made as sharply, jumps become less explosive and, most importantly, the technical aspect of a player's game will deteriorate rapidly.

In order to keep the intervals of work as intense as possible, start with a work/rest ratio between 5 to 1 and progress to a 4 to 1 ratio as your players become more fit.

Circuit # 1

Volume: Approximately 70% of 2,200 yards
Each sprint interval: 50 yards (there and back)
8 Sprints per station: 400 yards per station x 4 stations = 1,600 yards
Two Cones are placed 5 yards apart in the middle of each course.

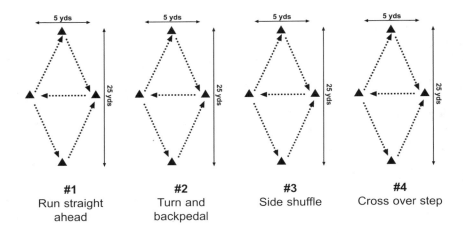

#1	#2	#3	#4
Run straight ahead	Turn and backpedal	Side shuffle	Cross over step

Players will run toward the right middle cone first when performing the designated footwork for that station. This insures that the players train the ability to both accelerate and decelerate going into and coming out of turns.

Using a roster of 20 players, you will have 5 players per station. Each player will run a predetermined number of sprints at each station. All the groups will start at the same time to insure that they end roughly at the same time as well.

After completing all their runs for a particular station, the entire team will participate in a jog around the entire soccer field as part of active recovery. This also helps build some camaraderie during what normally is the least popular aspect of a practice session.

Upon completion of the active recovery jog, each group will move on to the next station.

Circuit # 2

Volume: Approximately 70% of 2,200 yards
Each sprint interval: 50 yards (there and back)
8 Sprints per station: 400 yards per station x 4 stations = 1,600 yards

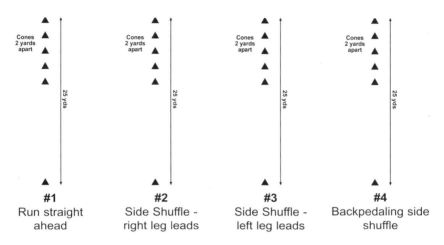

#1
Run straight ahead

#2
Side Shuffle - right leg leads

#3
Side Shuffle - left leg leads

#4
Backpedaling side shuffle

Players will sprint to the first cone and negotiate the 5 cones. They will run around the last cone and sprint straight back the full 30 yards.

Station 1:   Straight ahead running
Station 2:   Side shuffle-right legs leads
Station 3:   Side shuffle-left leg leads
Station 4:   Backpedaling side shuffle

Circuit # 3

Volume: Approximately 70% of 2,200 yards
Each sprint interval: 50 yards (there and back)
8 Sprints per station: 400 yards per station x 4 stations = 1,600 yards

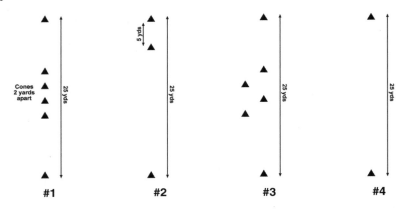

Station 1: Sprint to first cone, backpedal side shuffle through 4 middle cones, turn around, sprint to far cone, straight back sprint.

Station 2: Sprint to farthest cone, pick up med ball/soccer ball and hold it waist high close to your stomach, quickly side shuffle to near cone and back twice (4 lengths), put ball down by cone, sprint all the way back.

Station 3: Sprint to first cone and use any footwork necessary to go through 4 middle cones as fast as possible, sprint to far cone, staright sprint back.

Station 4: Sprint to far cone, jump up for 4 headers tossed by coach. If alone, just perform jumping headers w/out ball, sprint back

Zig - Zag Shuttles

Volume: Approximately 70% of 2,200 yards
Each sprint interval: 50 yards (there and back)
8 Sprints per station: 400 yards per station x 4 stations = 1,600 yards

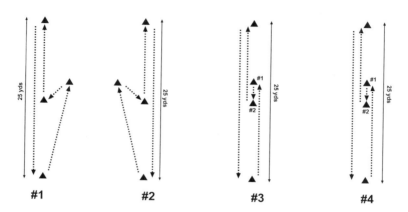

Center cones are approximately 4-5 yards apart.

Station 1:   Sprint to the right cone, backpedal to the center cone, sprint to far cone, straight sprint back.

Station 2:   Sprint to the left cone, backpedal to center cone, sprint to far cone, straight back sprint.

Station 3:   Sprint to cone #1, right leg lead side shuffle to cone #2, sprint to far cone, straight back sprint.

Station 4:   Sprint to cone #1, left leg lead side shuffle to cone #2, sprint to far cone, straight back sprint.

Conclusion

This chapter doesn't have all the answers. Like all other coaches, I've taken bits and pieces from fitness sessions I've witnessed, participated in or read about and applied exercise principles and some common sense. We can all come up with a fitness session that will leave our players bent over with exhaustion. Sports science can help us better use our time as coaches to get the most out of our players.

The two thoughts I'd like to leave you with are the importance of a proper warm up and cool down and listening to your players.

A proper warm up and cool down can significantly help reduce injuries. Don't be in a rush to get to the meat of your practice at the expense of a few extra minutes of warming up. Take the time to allow players to loosen up properly in order to give the maximum effort that will be required for the session. I can't think of a worse way to pull a muscle than in a hastily conducted warm-up session. My practices aren't over until we've finished cooling down and stretching. I know some coaches use the cool down to talk to players. I recommend you don't. If you are talking about team travel during the cool down period, players won't be giving their stretching the proper attention.

Don't be afraid to listen to your players. Many coaches like to be known as slave drivers and will dismiss all comments players make about over training. Proper rest is important and should be given serious consideration by planning your sessions weeks in advance. Staleness is normally caused by the over-training done over time and not over the previous couple of days.
The fatigue of a busy schedule of training and games will manifest itself a week or two after the fact. Properly planned rest will allow the body to constantly give maximum effort and reduce the risk of injuries.

SOCCER NUTRITION FOR PEAK PERFORMANCE
by Chris Ramsey

Over the past 20 years or so it has been acknowledged by the general public that good nutrition will have a beneficial effect on health and well being. In turn, this has impacted on the sports world. Competitive sportspeople have become aware that the role of nutrition can play a significant part in the enhancement of performance during training and competition.

The soccer world has generally taken a lethargic approach to implementing effective nutritional programs with their players. The consequences of this are that poor dietary habits often prevail. This in turn can have a major effect on a player's ability to maximize his fitness. Therefore it is important that coaches/players have a basic understanding of how sound nutritional habits can have a positive impact on performance.

To be ahead of the game, coaches/players need to have a working knowledge of these areas:

- What the food groups are
- What they do
- Where to find them
- How to use them to enhance performance
- There are differences with children
- Issues to be considered when dealing with female players

What are the food groups?

The food groups can be broken down into five areas: Macro-nutrients, Micro-nutrients, Vitamins, Minerals, and Fluids.

Macro-nutrients
Macro-nutrients are divided into three categories: carbohydrates (carbs), fats, and protein.

Carbohydrates
Carbohydrates are the body's preferred source of energy yielding

4 kcals per gram. It is the first nutrient to be called upon during any activity.

Carbohydrates are divided into two types, simple and complex. Simple carbs are used by the body more quickly than complex carbs, which take longer to breakdown. Complex carbs have a higher nutritional value as they contain minerals, vitamins, and fiber.

Whether simple or complex, carbs are broken down into a basic form known as glucose. Glucose is stored in the body in a form known as glycogen. The body maintains stores of glycogen in the muscles and liver. This store is used to maintain blood sugar level and ensure that the brain and muscles are constantly supplied with glucose.

Carbohydrates are used during prolonged aerobic activities such as jogging and anaerobic activities like sprinting. Once the carbs (glycogen) in the muscle have been used up the ability to run and sprint is reduced.

Fats
Although fats contain twice as many calories as carbohydrates, yielding 9 kcals per gram, they take longer to break down. Fats are not available for use during high intensity exercise such as sprinting. They are the body's second preferred energy choice. Fat is used in lower intensity aerobic work like jogging and walking. The body stores most of it's energy as fat in fatty tissues and muscle cells. For this reason a player should make sure that his fat intake is very well controlled.

Fats can be broken down into two types, saturated and unsaturated. Unsaturated fats contain essential fatty acids (cannot be manufactured by the body) and have a more positive effect on health than saturated.

Fat is important for long term energy production, endurance, cell membrane formation, brain tissue, nerve sheath, bone marrow, protection of vital organs, and the absorption of vitamins A,D,E and K.

Protein

Proteins (4 kcals per gram) are made up of twenty amino acids, of which eight are essential (cannot be manufactured by the body). The main functions of Proteins are growth and repair of the body, manufacture of hormones, enzymes, and assisting in the production of antibodies to fight infection. This nutrient is a minor energy source and only used as energy in extreme conditions when carbs are in limited supply.

Protein can also be divded into two categories, first and second class. First class proteins are found in meat, fish, and poultry. First class proteins contain all the essential amino acids needed by the body. Second class proteins can be found in a range of foods like grains, nuts, vegetables, and dairy products. Second class proteins do not contain all the essential amino acids. A variety of second class proteins is needed to provide all amino acids needed if the player is a vegetarian.

Fluids

Water provides many functions in the body. It is one of the body's most important nutrients. About 60% of the body's weight is made up of Water. All the cells in the body contain water and it is needed for transporting nutrients, gases, and helping to regulate the body's temperature.

During a match a player can lose between 2-3 litres of water through sweat. This can be detrimental as a loss of as little as 2% in body weight (water) can lead to a 10 - 20% deterioration in performance.

Players should attempt to stay hydrated constantly during the day, not just before and during activity. If a player becomes thirsty (s)he is already dehydrated and it becomes difficult to redress this deficit as the body can only absorb about a pint (600ml) per hour, or around 150ml every 15mins.

Sports Drinks have a dual function for soccer players, water replacement and carbohydrate replenishment. There are many sports drinks on the market and it is important to be aware that all sports drinks are not the same. The main difference between sports drinks is the rate at which they replenish water (hydrate) and/or carbohydrates.

Most modern sports drinks contain carbohydrates and electrolytes. Electrolytes are minerals found the body. They regulate fluid balances and assist with the absorption of water. Within the body there is a certain concentration of this combination (carbs' and electrolytes) that allows the body to function optimally. Sports drinks aim to redress the balance of the nutrients (water, electrolytes & carbohydrates) lost through exercise and sweat. The rate at which the water in these sports drinks is absorbed is dependent on the concentration of carbs and electrolytes in the drink compared to that of the body.

Sports drinks are broken into three main types; Hypotonic, hypertonic & isotonic. (See Table 1).

Drink Type	Concentration	Content	Absorption	When to Use
Water			150ml every 15 min.	At all times
Hypotonic	Less than the body	A small amount of carbs Electrolytes 2% or 2g (carbohydrate) per 100ml of water	Almost as quick as water	At all times
Hypertonic	Higher than the body	Electrolytes 10% + or 10g+ (carbohydrate) per 100ml of water	In excess of 20 min depending on the concentration	Best used in the recovery
Isotonic	The same as the body	Electrolytes Between 6-7% or 6-7g (carbohydrate) per 100 ml of water	Quicker than water	At all times

Players should restrict intake of alcohol and caffeinated drinks, such as soda, coffee, and tea. These drinks have a dehydrating effect.

Vitamins & Minerals

Vitamins and minerals are needed to assist in regulating processes in the body such as growth, fluid balance in the tissues, and general health. Vitamins and minerals do not directly provide energy and are required in very small quantities. A balanced diet should provide a player with the correct amount needed. In some cases it may be necessary for players to consume a multi - vitamin in order to be sure they have met their requirements as many minerals and vitamins can be lost in cooking and food preparation.

Where can they be found?
What do they do?

Nutrient	Function	Where Found
Carbohydrate *Simple:* These are found in refined foods. (sugar) *Complex:* These are found in natural unrefined foods. Generally hard to break down and need a lot of chewing.	Body's first choice as fuel for energy Used to maintain constant bodily functins and blood sugar levels.	*Simple carbs:* Sugar, candy, jelly, chocolate, soda, cookies, etc. *Complex carbs:* Grains, cereals, pasta, oatmeal, rice, bread, fruit, vegetables.

Nutrient	Function	Where Found
Fats *Saturated:* Mainly found in animal fats and are usually solid at room temperature *Unsaturated:* Essential fatty acid. Mainly liquid at room temperature.	Unsaturated fats have more positive effect on health than saturated. These essential fatty acids are extremely important to the diet. Needed for long term energy and absorption of vitamins A, D, E, and K.	*Saturated:* Butter, cheese, lard *Unsaturated:* Olive oil, fish oil, nuts
Protein *1st Class:* Meat, poultry, fish *2nd Class:* Dairy products, pulses, grains	Repair, growth, manufacture of hormones and enzymes	*1st Class:* Steak, chicken, salmon, tuna *2nd Class:* Pasta, beans, soy, nuts, rice, cheese, yogurt, milk
Vitamins and Minerals	Regulatory and structural roles: fluid balance, bone structure, nerve function, formation of enzymes, hormones, etc.	A balanced diet should provide the minerals needed. The inclusion of fruit and vegetables in the diet will add many of the vitamins and minerals needed. Five portions a day is generally recommended

How can soccer players use diet to improve performance?

- Eat a carbohydrate rich diet, with a mixture of complex and simple (mainly complex).
- Ensure that fruit and vegetables are part of the diet.
- The diet must contain foods that have some fibre, such as grains and fruit. Fibre helps the smooth digestion of food.
- Cut down on fatty foods like fries, chips, pies, cheese, cream.
- Drink at least 8 cups (150ml) of water a day. More during activity
- Check sports drinks. If uncertain drink water.
- Eat simple carbohydrates (low fat) at the end of a session / match as they are absorbed quickly and start the recovery process straight away.
- Snack sensibly between meals with healthy options such as fruit and selected cereal bars
- Steer away from simple carbs in the build up to activity. Simple carbs rapidly increase blood sugar, this is followed by a drastic drop in the blood sugar level which leaves the player feeling tired and lethargic.
- Do not rely solely on the pre-match meal to provide all the energy for the game, as glycogen stores may be low by that stage and the pre-match meal may only partially restore glycogen levels rather than providing energy for the entire match.
- Carbohydrate loading in soccer refers to increasing carbohydrate consumption 28 - 48 hours before a game in order to maximize glycogen reserves. This can help ensure that there is an ample amount of energy available for a match.
- Remember, mixing foods can change the nutritional balance of a meal. For example, putting too much fatty sauces on foods can mean that you are actually consuming more fat than protein or Carbohydrate.
- A player's diet should consist of a balance of; 60% Carbohydrate, 25% Fat & 15% protein. On a diet of 2000 kilo calories this would mean 300 grams of carbohydrate, approx' 54 grams of fat, and 75 grams of protein in day.

THE PRE-MATCH MEAL

In order to get maximum benefit from the pre-match meal it should:

- Be consumed at least 3 hours before the game to enable sufficient time for digestion.
- Contain mainly complex Carbohydrates, like rice or pasta, a small amount of protein, like grilled chicken or fish, and salad, vegetables or fruit in moderation.
- Include plenty of hydrating fluids such as water, diluted sports drinks and diluted juices.

What should be avoided
- A heavy meal. For example a meal that leaves you so full that you are in discomfort. This may cause slow Digestion.
- Large amounts of protein e.g steak and pork can take up to four hours to digest.
- Fatty foods, as they slow down digestion.
- Drinks with too much carbohydrate (over 10%)
- The intake of refined sugars. Common table sugar and confectionary are the most obvious.
- Caffeinated drinks like tea, coffee, soda, some sports drinks should be limited as they are diuretic and cause the body to lose water.
- Alcohol, as it has a negative effect on endurance, power, strength, and co- ordination. Alcohol is also a diuretic and causes dehydration.
- Salt tablets actually slow the hydrating process. The best way to replace salt is either through food or drinks that contain electrolytes.

POST MATCH

- Consume simple carbs as soon as activity/match is over (with in 2 hours) . Simple carbs are absorbed quicker than complex, but even quicker within the first 2 hours.
- Drink as much fluid as possible. This is where sports drinks of all kinds can freely be used to encourage hydration and carb replenishment.
- Avoid alcohol and caffeinated drinks, especially in the first two hours as they are diuretic and encourage the loss of water.
- Continue to drink fluids and consume carbs periodically (every 2hrs) in order to continue glycogen replenishment and recovery.

FACTORS CONCERNING CHILDREN

It is important to realize that there are certain factors that need to be highlighted when dealing with the nutrition of young players.

- A child's temperature is not regulated as efficiently as an adult's. Therefore they tend to overheat more quickly. During sessions water breaks should be frequent (every 15 mins or less in hot conditions).
- Junk foods should generally not be encouraged as they contain a lot of fat, refined sugar, and rarely have nutrients needed by the body.
- Junk food also contributes to un-necessary body fat and dental problems.
- However; junk food can sometimes be used in a positive way if there is the need to consume a lot of carbohydrate in a short time (post activity/ between games at a tournament). For instance simple sugars in low fat candy e.g. gummy bears are easy to digest and absorbed quickly.
- During tournaments, fruits such as grapes, peaches, bananas may be used to help the recovery and assist in hydration as they are easily digested and contain large amounts of water and sugar.

- Hypertonic sports drinks are also a way of consuming a lot of carbohydrate between games at a tournament. A regulated amount will lead to quick absorption and also mean that the player avoids the discomfort of having to digest solid food.
- Unless a child is unwell a special diet is not necessary. Adults may restrict certain foods because of the fat content. It is important to be aware that some foods that contain fat (e.g dairy products) are essential for growth in children.
- Children should not participate in activity when they are hungry. Children process food quickly; therefore they can afford to eat closer to a match than recommended for adults.

FEMALE PLAYERS

Many young females are influenced by western society's view of beauty and occasionally take dieting too far. A coach must be aware that extreme diets can leave the player deficient of essential nutrients. In women this can manifest itself in some of the following problems;

- Having a body fat level that is too low, which can lead to a menstrual cycle problem called Amenorrhoea. This where the cycle is affected so severely that it can stop.
- Striving to obtain very low body fat can sometimes mean that certain foods e.g diary products are neglected. This means that minerals such as calcium are not consumed, which can lead to growth problems and contribute in the development of osteoporosis later on in life.
- Eating disorders like anorexia and bulimia can lead to poor health. These disorders occur when a person eats very little or not at all (Anorexia), or when a person eats but immediately after the meal makes herself vomit, thus dispelling the food from the body (Bulimia). Both disorders prevent the body from obtaining necessary nutrients. One major problem here is the lack of Iron intake. Iron is needed for energy production and the formation of red blood cells.
- Some tell tale signs are; rapid weight loss, mood changes, excessive muscle cramps, loss of appetite.

PART 5
SESSIONS

Big Box, Little Box
Psychological and Technical Warm Up

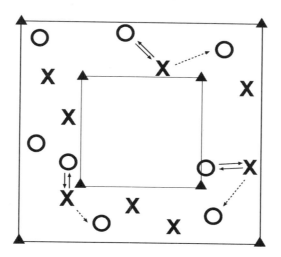

ORGANIZATION
- 30x30 yard grid with a 15x15 yard grid inside.
- Each player has a partner and each pair has a ball.
- Players spread out over the 30x30 yards.

OBJECTIVE
- To warm up the players prior to the main activity at the beginning of practice by performing various techniques.
- One player remains static and acts as a server, while the other moves around from server to server.
- On the Coach's call, the players move quickly from the large box to the small box, varying the movement and sharpening their decision making.

COACHING POINTS
- Sharpness of technique performed.
- How quickly do the players react mentally between the two grids?
- Stretch between various technique performed.

Circle Warm Up #1

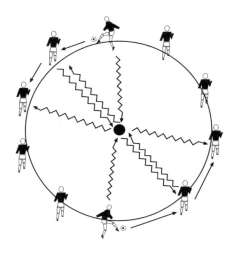

ORGANIZATION
- Around the center circle
- 12-16 players with 2 balls between them

OBJECTIVE
To warm up in a more dynamic setting, keeping all players moving.

COACHING POINTS
- All players begin by facing out away from the center.
- The players who start with the ball are at opposite ends of the circle. They begin by passing with the left foot (inside of foot) to the player closest to them and jog into the center.
- The player receiving receives with his right foot (inside of foot) and plays it to the next player with his left and then also jogs into the center of the circle.
- When they jog back they come back to the next player's place which means they have moved on one.
- This goes on until players have returned to their starting point.

VARIATION
Play with the right and receive with the left, facing in towards the center.

ORGANIZATION
- 12-16 players
- 2 balls
- Start at opposite sides.

OBJECTIVE
To warm up and stretch, keeping the players together.

COACHING POINTS
- All players face outwards.
- Play with the left, receive with the right.
- Turn and jog into the middle.
- Back out to the next player's place moving on one spot after each pass and jog all the way round.
- Reverse the drill: play with the right and receive with the left.

Circle Warm Up #2

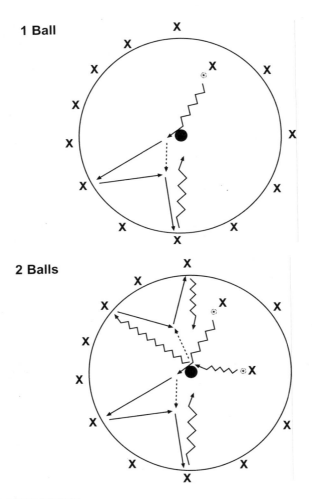

ORGANIZATION
12-16 players around the center circle, 3-4 balls.

OBJECTIVE
To warm up and practice on some basic passing techniques.

ACTION
- Player in possession dribbles across the circle
- When he reaches half way he calls out a name and passes to that player.
- That player passes back to the player who began with the ball, who then passes to another player who repeats the process.

VARIATION
Use a number of balls depending on the number of players and their skill level.

VARIATION
Passing with different areas of the foot.

VARIATION
Receiving 1 touch or 2 touch.

ORGANIZATION & OBJECTIVE
Same as before

ACTION
- Here we want the players on either side of the player who's name is called to switch with each other.
- The named player passes the ball back to the original player who then plays to one of the two who switched.
- That player repeats the process.

COACHING POINTS
Encourage communication, vision, speed of play and concentration by the players to keep it moving correctly.

Technical Warm Up #1

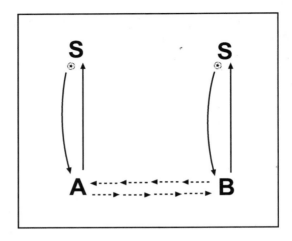

ORGANIZATION
- 10 yd box
- 4 players
- 4 cones
- 2 balls

OBJECTIVE
To warm up focusing on some basic techniques.

COACHING POINTS
(Technical Activity)
- Servers don't move.
- Players A & B move side to side facing S and perform same technique back to the server: heading, volleying, side foot volley, chest and volley, head and volley, thigh and volley, etc.
- Change A & B with server.

Technical Warm Up #2

ORGANIZATION
- 2 players
- 1 ball
- Three cones 5 yds apart

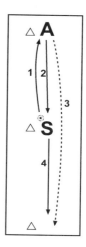

OBJECTIVE
To warm up focusing on basic techniques at the same time.

COACHING POINTS
(Technical Activity)
- Server stands at middle cones.
- Player A stands at one of the others.
- S serves to A.
- A plays ball back using a specific technique, then jogs to the other cone behind S.
- S then serves the ball again for player A to repeat.
- Server can vary service and technique: half volleys, chest and pass, thigh and volley etc.

Technical Warm Up #3

ORGANIZATION
- 40 x 30 yards
- 16 players
- 1 ball between 2.

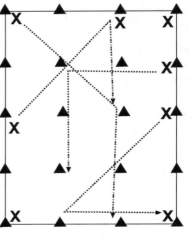

OBJECTIVE
To warm up and focus on some basic techniques.

COACHING POINTS
- Players with the ball are static and serve the ball when called for by a specific player.
- The static player can either hold it in his hands or pass with his feet. It will depend upon the exercise or technique to be performed.
- Once the player has played the ball back to the server he must change direction and call out again and repeat the process.
- After a few minutes the players switch with their partner, stretch and repeat.
- Heading, chesting, volleying, 1-2 takeovers, overlaps, etc.

Grid Warm Ups

ORGANIZATION
- 20 yard grid, 10 x 5 yard box inside grid.
- 4 groups of players divided up equally behind each of the cones in the smaller grid.

OBJECTIVE
To warm up in a dynamic setting while getting touches on the ball and sprinting.

COACHING POINTS FIG A
- Play it forward to player facing you.
- After you play it, sprint to the cone placed on the outside of grid on the same side as the team facing you.

COACHING POINTS FIG B
- Play it forward to player facing you.
- After you play it, run diagonally around the cone at the far corner and join the team that is diagonal to you.
- Again, sprint - ¾ to full.

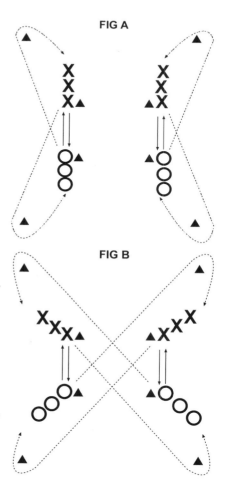

Warm Up for Team Shape

ORGANIZATION
- 30 x 40 yds
- 11 v 11
- Supply of balls.

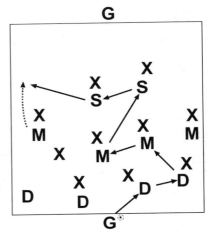

OBJECTIVE (HANDBALL)
To get players in a formation, 4-4-2 for example, and move up the field to the other end, passing the ball through each other, staying in shape until the team in possession can pass to the goalkeeper at the other end.

COACHING POINTS
- Maintain shape while in transition.
- Keep compact while in transition.
- Communication and movement off the ball.
- Defensive shape when not in possession.
- Offensive shape when in possession.

Warm Up for Possession

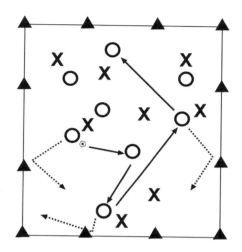

ORGANIZATION
- 50 x 30 yds
- 16 players split into 2 teams
- 1 ball

OBJECTIVE
- To quicken the players' reaction by placing cones on the outside of the marked grid.
- After a player passes the ball to one of his teammates, he must touch a cone at the edge of the playing area before he can get back into the game. Failure to do so will result in the player's team and himself being penalized.

COACHING POINTS
- Speed of player's reaction after he has played the ball.
- Player running hard and getting his lungs working.
- Encourages players to move their heads to see where nearest cone is.
- Also helps players create space, if they tend to play tight.
- Also can be used as a good fitness activity.
- Gets players' brains working more quickly as they look for a way of beating the activity.

INTRODUCTION TO PRESSING

The number one reason for a goal being scored is:
"There is no pressure on the ball."

When a player decides to put pressure on the ball, we call it pressing. Loosely explained, pressing is getting pressure on the ball. Limiting the opponent's passing options, denying his ability to penetrate, either with or without the ball, and winning back possession of the ball are all reasons for pressing. An individual player can pressure the ball effectively if he is trying to accomplish the following:

1. Deny penetration, slow down his decision making.
2. Limit the opponent's options by forcing him in one direction.
3. Force the opponent to make an error.
4. Win the ball back.

However, when pressing collectively within a small group, you gain a significant advantage over your opponent if you are effective in your implementation. Identifying at the correct moment when to press enables you some of these benefits:

1. Isolating your opponent to gain a numbers up advantage.
2. Denying penetration.
3. Squeezing the space of your opponent, limiting his options.
4. Forcing your opponent to turn the ball over.
5. Working within the group enables the pressing player to be given cover and balance by the supporting players

When a team includes pressing as part of their tactics, the responsibility will always come down to the player closest to the ball. Should he go? Should he bend his run one way or the other? Can he get to the player in possession quickly enough to be effective? If he does go to the ball, will he be supported by his teammates giving cover, balance and depth where needed? Understanding the roles of the 1st, 2nd and 3rd defenders will make pressing simpler.

Ultimately the goal is to win the ball back.

Pressing 1
3 Team Pressing

ORGANIZATION
- 40 x 60 yds
- 2 Goalkeepers, 12 players, 4 reds, 4 blues, 4 whites.

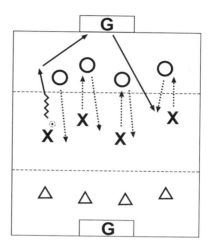

OBJECTIVE
- 4 players defend and 4 attack.
- When attack finishes with a shot on goal or it breaks down, the defending team counters in the opposite direction and the attacking team defends.
- All 3 teams rotate in order.
- Defenders must stay in defensive third.

COACHING POINTS
- Getting pressure on the ball as soon as it gets into the defensive third,
- The rest of the defense provides cover and balance to pressing players (defense)
- Communication.

Pressing 2
Man for Man Pressing

ORGANIZATION
- 40 x 60 yard area
- 16 players, 8 v 8, 2 Goalkeepers,
- 8 red and 8 whites.

OBJECTIVE
- Players man mark each other.
- The objective is to not allow your man to get clear and score.
- This will create pressing assignments all over the field.

COACHING POINTS
- Don't allow your man to score.
- Provide support and cover when necessary.
- Get pressure on the ball as soon as possible.

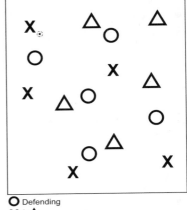

O Defending
X + △ in Possession

Pressing 3
When to Press

ORGANIZATION
- 20 x 40 yards
- 15 players, 5 v 5 v 5
- Supply of balls

OBJECTIVE
When a team loses possession, it must identify when to press and where to win the ball back. It is important that a team work on this decision making progress together, so that they can learn together to recognize specific visual cues which should act as triggers.

COACHING POINTS
When to press:
- When a player drops his head with the ball and you are close enough to tackle.
- When you have identified a weak player on the opposition and he has gained possession or has a poor 1st touch.
- When the ball is played in behind a defender who is facing his own goal and you are close enough to apply pressure preventing him to turn.
- When the ball is in the air and traveling.
- When you have numbers up.

Pressing 4
Pressure, Cover and Balance

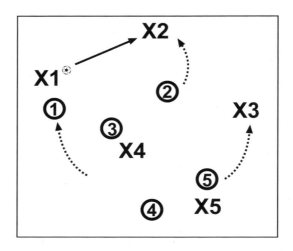

ORGANIZATION
- 20 x 20 yds
- 10 players, 5 v 5
- Supply of balls

OBJECTIVE
To train the players who are in a supporting role how to cover at the correct distance and how they balance together, keeping compact behind the ball.

COACHING POINTS
- Recognizing specific triggers (visual and verbal cues):
- Player in possession drops his head.
- Ball is played to a player in a difficult situation, i.e. facing away from his teammates.
- Player in possession has no support (numbers down).
- Player closest to the player in possession is close enough to step and tackle him.
- Supporting players are compact behind the pressing player, providing the correct depth and balance.
- Communication.

ACTION

- X1 is in possession.
- Os have to press him towards X2 in order to eventually win the ball.
- The key in this exercise is to get Os players into a position to provide the correct cover and balance.
- O1 forces X1 to play to X2.
- O2 bends his run to take X3 and X5 out of the picture.
- O1 steps inside of X to mark him out, leaving Os 3, 4 and 5 to provide cover and balance and also get compact behind the pressing players.

Pressing 5

ORGANIZATION
- 20 x 40 yds
- 12 players, 4 v 4 & 4, 4 reds, 4 blues and 4 whites
- Supply of balls

OBJECTIVE
- 4 wall players have 2 touches and only play with the team who has possession of the ball.
- When the team that is in possession loses the ball, the coach will time that team on how quickly they can regain possession of the ball.
- The team in possession will count out how many consecutive passes they can make.
- The team with the highest number of passes and the shortest time to regain possession wins.

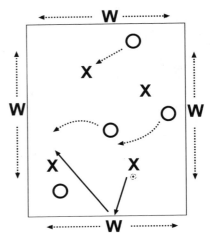

COACHING POINTS
- Closest man to the player in possession must press the ball.
- The rest of the team must verbally instruct him to press, as they provide cover and balance of the shape of the player pressing.
- Recognition of visual cues of the player pressing, i.e. body shape, body direction, how close he is to player in possession.
- Pressing player must trust information being passed to him from his teammates.
- Communication must be clear, concise and short.
- Os need to pick the correct moment to step or press or they could be chasing for a long period of time.

Pressing 6
8 v 4

ORGANIZATION
- 20 x 40 yds
- 16 players, 8 v 8

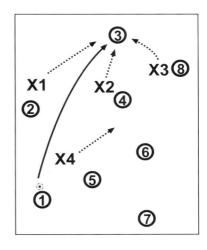

OBJECTIVE
To get the 4 players that are working together to apply high pressure
for 2 minutes and try to get as
many interceptions as they can.
They then switch with 4 players
from the group of 8.
Repeat the process.

COACHING POINTS
- Recognizing the correct time as an individual and as a group to
  step to the ball to be effective in pressing.
- Effective communication. Short, sharp information on when to
press, where to cover and how to balance.
- How to reorganize and work effectively as a group.

ACTION
- O1 plays a long ball past O3 who controls it.
- While the ball is in the air, the Xs decide to press because the
ball is played in behind O3 and
not only is O3 their weakest player technically but the Os are
also numbers down in that situation.
- Xs now move into pressing mode and press through Xs 1, 2
and 3.
- X4 adds balance and cover.

INTRODUCTION TO POSSESSION

I cannot stress enough how important it is that a player develops the skills necessary to maintain possession of the ball under the tightest of situations. With more and more teams using pressing tactics, if a player loses possession of the ball he will be finished. There are many coaching points in learning to keep the ball: A good first touch, Playing away from pressure, Keeping the pass simple, Setting up angles for passes, Continuous movement to supporting players on the ball to give the players in possession a number of options, Effective communication (verbal and visual), Knowing when to release the ball, and knowing when to hold the ball. However, for me, the most important thing is knowing when to penetrate. Possession must have a purpose and that purpose is preparing to penetrate. If you do not penetrate at the precise moment, you will not create scoring opportunities.

I was recently talking to a highly respected soccer coach after a professional game and he said to me, "Where have all the good soccer players gone?" He was directly addressing the way that both teams had failed to keep possession of the ball under the slightest pressure from the opposition. I am of the opinion that we do not put enough pressure on our players to really work hard at keeping possession of the ball, especially in match conditions. Possession is a crucial component in the development of every player and to every team's system of play. These possession activities are simple, dynamic, and at the same time will continuously challenge your players.

Possession
Creating Better Angles

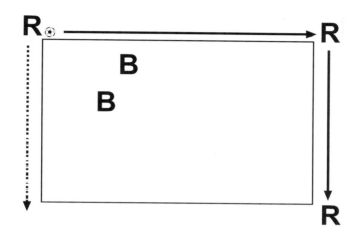

ORGANIZATION
- 10 x 10 yards
- 3 v 2, 3 reds and 2 blues
- Supply of balls.

OBJECTIVE
- To maintain possession of the ball with only two touches.
- The 3 reds who are just outside the 10 yard box must keep the ball moving and they can move around the outside of the box freely.
- They cannot enter the box.
- If they pass across the box and it is intercepted they lose a point.
- They must move for each other to create angles for passes.

COACHING POINTS
- Players must move quickly to create angles.
- Their first touch needs to be towards support and they must anticipate the next pass.

Variation

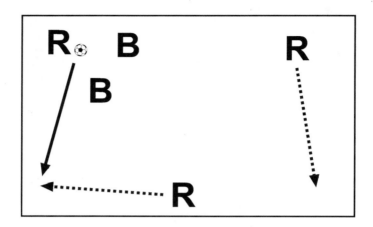

ORGANIZATION
- 10 x 10 yds
- 3 v 2, 3 reds and 2 blues
- Supply of balls.

OBJECTIVE
Same as before except the reds are now inside the box and cannot move outside it.

COACHING POINTS
- Players have to pass and move more quickly.
- Their first touch needs to be away from pressure, and support players need to become available sooner.
- Communication plays a bigger part now.

Possession
4+4 v 4+4

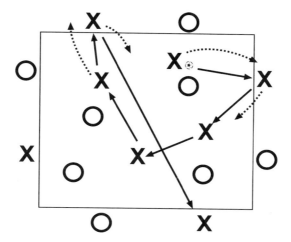

ORGANIZATION
- 40 x 40 yds
- Supply of balls around grid
- 16 players, 8Xs, 8Os
- Two touch only
- 4 players from each team around the grid, 4 players in the inside.

OBJECTIVE
- To maintain possession of the ball with two touches.
- When the team has possession, they can play to an outside player who has two touches.
- When they are played to, they must enter the field of play and switch with the player who passed to them.
- A fast exchange of players and passes is expected.

COACHING POINTS
- Angle of passes to the players on the outside of the grid.
- First touch should be inside away from pressure.
- Quick combination passes between players.
- Maintaining possession is critical.

Possession
4 v 4+8 wall players

ORGANIZATION
- 20 x 40 yds
- 16 players, 4 reds, 4 blues, 8 wall players
- Supply of balls.

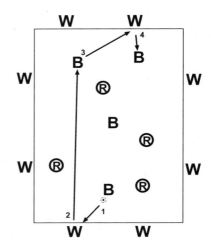

OBJECTIVE
- For the blue team or red team to maintain possession with the aid of the white team who are playing as wall players.
- Wall players have two touches and cannot be tackled.

COACHING POINTS
- Angle at which player receives the ball from wall player
- Movement of support from teammates
- When to play longer passes and why.

VARIATION
1. Every 3rd pass must be played to a wall player.
2. Restriction on touches: 2 touch, unlimited touches.

Possession
8 v 4+4

ORGANIZATION
- 40 x 20 yds
- 16 players, 8 blues, 4 reds, 4 whites
- No restrictions on touches to start.
- Supply of balls.

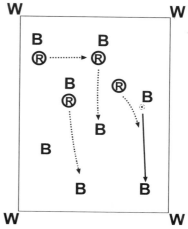

OBJECTIVE
- For the blue team to maintain possession of the ball from the red team.
- If the red team wins possession, they can use the white team players, who are on all 4 corners, to help them keep the ball.

COACHING POINTS
- Angle of support
- Pace of the pass
- Keeping the ball moving
- Playing out of tight and pressured areas.

VARIATION
Restrict touches on the ball: 2 touch for blue team, 1 touch for white team, unlimited touches for red team.

Possession

8 v 8

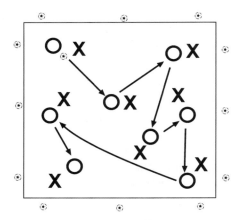

ORGANIZATION

- 40 x 40 yard grid
- 16 players, 8 v 8, two touch (mandatory)
- 8 yellows and 8 reds
- Supply of balls placed around the outside of the area
- 8 consecutive passes = 1 goal.

OBJECTIVE

- To get the players to maintain possession of the ball.
- Also, to get players to move the ball and create passing angles for option for the player in possession.
- Play mandatory two touch so the 1st touch must be away from pressure.

COACHING POINTS

- First touch must be away from pressure.
- Player receiving the ball needs to have a look behind to assess his options before he receives the ball.
- Angle of body when receiving pass.
- Movement of player after the player has passed the ball.

INTRODUCTION TO TRANSITIONAL PLAY

The speed at which a team transitions from defense to offense really depends on two key factors. The first factor is physical. A player must be physically fit to play both sides of the ball. The second factor is psychological. A player has to be psychologically prepared to do the work. Players constantly need to evolve to keep pace with the demands of the game. Speed of thought and speed of play are crucial if you are to be competitive with your counterparts.

By creating a competitive environment for your players in recreating match play with transitional activities, you are preparing them physically and psychologically for the demands of the game. I use many of these transitional activities early on in the season to help create good training habits. Being able to react immediately if you have won or lost possession of the ball enables you to become more effective as an individual and as a team. The other obvious benefit is that it doubles as a good fitness exercise with the ball. These activities help build aerobic and anaerobic fitness.

Transition 1
4 v 4

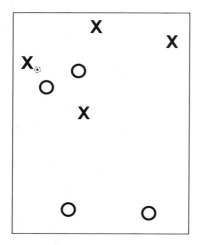 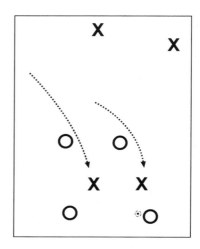

ORGANIZATION
- 20 x 40 yds
- 8 players, 4 v 4
- 4 reds, 4 blues.
- Supply of balls

OBJECTIVE
- In one half of the grid, X plays 4 v 2, 2 Os in the other half.
- Once the defending pair wins possession of the ball, they have to play it immediately to their teammates in the next half.
- The closest 2 players from the opposition step up and press the ball as quickly as possible.

COACHING POINTS
- How quickly does the defending team transition to attack?
- How quickly does the attacking team step up and press the ball as it transitions to defense?

Transition 2
Possession Activities

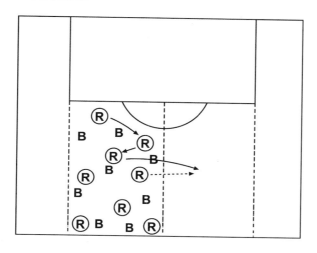

ORGANIZATION
- From the edge of the goal area to the half way line, mark off with cones and divide into 2 halves
- Split players into 8 v 8, 8 reds, 8 blues.
- Supply of balls on outside of area to keep play moving.

OBJECTIVE
For a team to transition from one half of the coned off area into the other half by moving the ball into that area for a player from the team in possession to run onto.

COACHING POINTS
- All players must be in one half of the grid.
- Look to release pressure from the opposition by playing into the other half for a player to run onto.
- Timing of run into the opposite half.
- Timing of pass.
- Type of run: flat, diagonal, bending, or on the dribble.
- Type of pass: lofted, driven, swerved.

Transition 3
5 v 5

ORGANIZATION
- 20 x 40 yds
- 10 players, 5 v 5,
- 5 reds, 5 blues.
- Supply of balls

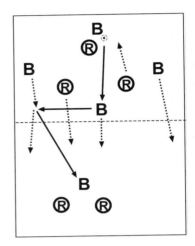

OBJECTIVE
- To help players recognize their immediate responsibility as the ball turns over from an attacking mode to a defensive mode.
- The role of the 1st, 2nd and 3rd defender come into play as well as the 1st, 2nd and 3rd attacker.

ADDED OBJECTIVES
- There should always be 4 v 3 on one side of the grid when it is the appropriate time.
- Keep possession until you can play it in the other half, keeping possession and making it 4 v 3 in the other half.
- If the defenders win the ball, the closest 3 players press and the closest team member joins in attack to make it 4 v 3.
- At that time, the furthest defender away from the ball drops into the other half to make it 1 v 2 in that half.

COACHING POINTS
- At the precise moment the ball turns over, how effectively do players transition from attack to defense and defense to attack.
- Communication between players is key to effectively recognize the roles of each of the players, i.e. 1st, 2nd and 3rd defenders or 1st, 2nd and 3rd attackers.

Transition 4
6 v 6+6

ORGANIZATION
- 40 x 60 yds
- 18 players and 2 goalkeepers
- 6 v 6 with targets and wingers
- Supply of balls.

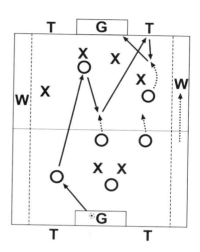

OBJECTIVE
- Through quick combination play transitioning from 4 v 2 in defensive half to 4 v 4 with targets and wingers in attacking half to create a numbers up to create scoring opportunities. This movement will cause a 2 v 2 in the defensive zone, players picking up man to man.
- After the attacking move has broken down or has been completed with a shot on goal, the two closest players transition back into their own defensive half, leaving the two closest players to the ball to press.

COACHING POINTS
- Create as many scoring opportunities as possible through quick combinations and identify the appropriate moment to transition.
- When defending, getting the right players to press the ball, delay the attack just long enough to enable the two closest players to get back and support the other defenders.

VARIATION
Play 6 v 6 straight up with wingers and targets.

Transition 5
Counter Attacking Game

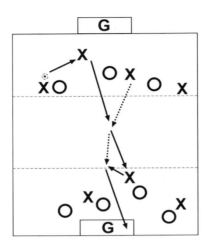

ORGANIZATION
- 40 x 60 yards divided into 3 equal thirds
- 14 field players and 2 goalkeepers, 4 defenders and 3 attackers in opposite ends
- No defenders allowed inside the middle third unless transitioning to attackers.

OBJECTIVE
- To transition from 4 defenders to 4 attackers via combination play through the middle third.
- When attack breaks down or finishes, the weak side attacker that is closest to his defenders transitions back immediately.
- The team that is now in possession of the ball attacks the goal at the opposite end.

COACHING POINTS
- Quick transitional counter attacks,
- Quick combinations to release attacking player
- Quick/fast recovery runs.

VARIATION

This time when the attacker transitions forward, one of the attackers can come short to create a passing option. When this happens, his defensive counterpart can move in as well.

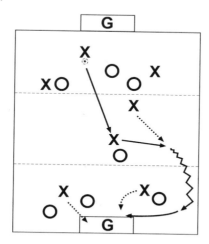

INTRODUCTION TO BLOCK DEFENDING

Block defending is a variation of zone defending. I have found that by teaching players their responsibilities while playing within a unit (block), it is easy for them to understand roles. Block defending can be used in various formations. As long as you can break down the responsibilities and roles of the units involved in working together, block defending can apply. Remember that for-mations and tactics will change, but the principles that govern the game stay the same (principle of defense). The principles of defending in blocks are; pressure, deny penetration, balance, compactness and depth. These principles will be implemented to the fullest when you are playing within blocks.

When implementing the structure of block defending, begin by breaking down your defensive responsibilities by the thirds of the field. When in your defensive third, you will want to show your opponent down the line and away from the goal. There are sev-eral reasons for you to do this.

1. Show your opponent away from your goals.
2. You can use the sideline as an additional defender.
3. By showing the opponent down the line, away from goal, you create additional recovery time and space for your teammates to get back in behind the ball.

In your midfield and attacking thirds of the field, you would want to show your opponent inside towards the field. The reasoning behind this is as follows:

1. You are showing the player towards a congested area.
2. You are showing the player into an area where you have addi-tional support and cover.
3. You can also train your players to invite the ball into specific areas that have been pre-selected before you step up to win the ball.
4. When their goalkeeper is in possession of the ball, you can give them the flanks to begin with by keeping your players out of there. By doing so, you can decide where you want your line of confrontation.

Block Defending 1

4 v 4 - Laying the Foundations

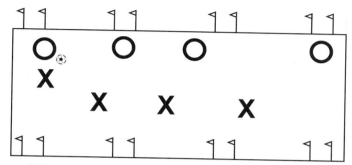

FIG 1 - Pressure the ball, show inside towards pressure

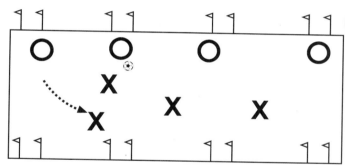

FIG 2 - Deny penetration, bend runs, apply pressure

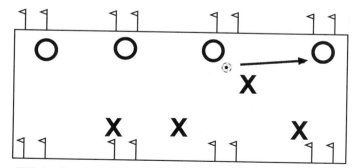

FIG 3 - Bend runs to deny penetration, as the ball travels so does pressure, other players provide support and balance

ORGANIZATION
- 10 x 40 yds
- 4 defenders and 4 midfielders
- Supply of balls
- 8 flags.

OBJECTIVE
- To organize your defenders and midfielders into defensive blocks.
- Keep players compact at all times, working on the principles of pressure, cover and balance.
- Also, to develop a rhythm of movement between the players within the blocks and to work on the overall communication.
- Player in possession tries to play through the block.

COACHING POINTS
- Get pressure on the ball by denying penetration first.
- Give cover to pressing player.
- Players bending runs to cover and deny penetration.
- As the ball travels, so does pressure.
- Proper distance and angle of balancing players.
- Defenders show away from the center, towards the side line.
- Midfielders show towards the center, towards pressure.

Block Defending 2
8 v 8 Building Blocks

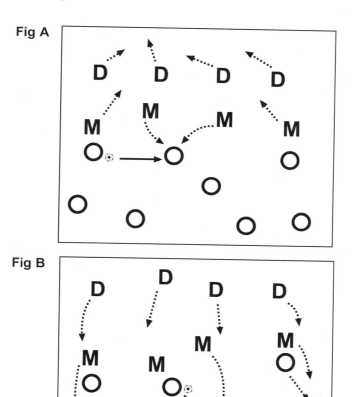

ORGANIZATION

- 40 x 40 yds
- 16 players divided into 2 teams of 8, with 4 defenders and 4 midfielders in each team
- Supply of balls,.

OBJECTIVE

- Organize your defenders and midfielders to work and move together as one,
- Keeping your blocks compact at all times, vertically and laterally
- To recognize, as a group, when to step together when pressing the ball.
- To communicate effectively with each other to develop a rhythm of movement.

COACHING POINTS

- Immediate pressure on the ball.
- The closest person giving the appropriate cover, distance, angle, etc.
- Balance of surrounding players and the economy of movement.
- Denying penetration by bending runs first before applying pressure.
- Effective communication between the pressing, covering and balancing players.
- Begin at a walking pace so players can see the blocks working.
- Freeze play and evaluate the shape, runs, etc.

Block Defending 3
Creating Counter Attack Options

ORGANIZATION
- 70 x 40 yard grid divided into thirds of 15-40-15 yards with 2 full size goals
- 18 players divided into 8 v 8 plus 2 goalkeepers,
- 4 midfielders from each team in middle third and 2 strikers and
- 2 defenders in end thirds
- Supply of balls

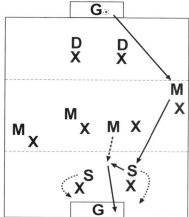

OBJECTIVE
- After regaining possession of the ball, look to create attacking options with quick combinations from midfield to strikers in final third.
- Emphasis will be on penetrating passes and third man running off the ball.
- Up to 2 midfielders can enter final third in support of strikers, creating numbers up.
- Defending midfielders in middle third cannot, at this stage, track back into defensive third.

COACHING POINTS
- Possession with a purpose to create space and passing seams.
- To penetrate at the correct moment with and without the ball.
- Timing of the support runs from midfield need to be on.
- Mobility and creative movements from the strikers.
- Progress by adding 2 full backs and go 11 v 11, full field.

Block Defending 4
Attacking and Counter Attacking Block Game

ORGANIZATION
- 2/3s of the field
- 3 fullsize goals, 2 placed 5 yards in on the edge of the defensive third side line, the other at the opposite end of the field.
- 14 players and 3 goalkeepers divided into 6 v 8, numbers down

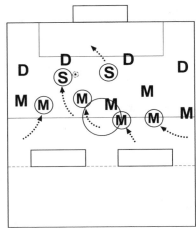

OBJECTIVE
- To initiate high pressure tactics from the front 2 strikers, adding appropriate support from midfield, while still limiting penetration.
- If the 8 players who are playing in their shape can mount an attack, they can score in the goal on the flanks in the final third.

COACHING POINTS
- 2 strikers working together to close down and take away options.
- Strikers and midfielders working together to deny penetration.
- The correct cover and balance provided by the additional players.
- When to step and press at the appropriate moment on visual and verbal cues.
- Compactness behind the player pressing is key.
- When implementing a pressing tactic, you first need to identify where your point of confrontation is going to be.
- The higher up the field you press, the more you will invite the opposition to play longer balls from the back. You must be aware of this and be comfortable with it.

Block Defending 5
Defending Block Game

ORGANIZATION
- 40 x 75 yd grid in the middle third of the field
- 16 players divided into 2 teams of 8, 4 defenders and 4 mid-fielders in each team
- Supply of balls
- 6 sets of flags

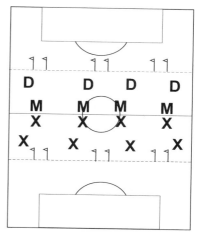

OBJECTIVE
- To defend effectively in the blocks, maintaining the team shape, keeping the blocks compact and working as one block.
- After winning the ball back, objective changes to stretching your opponent lengthwise and width wise, making it difficult for the other team to reorganize into their shape.

COACHING POINTS
- Compactness behind the ball.
- Speed of the blocks balancing and shifting together.
- Speed of the counter attack after regaining possession.
- Speed of the blocks to shrink the field down,
- Playing within the blocks,
- Giving the opposition no options.
- Both teams try to score in the goals (poles 5 yards apart).

INTRODUCTION TO SPEED OF PLAY

Speed of play is a buzz phrase that entered into the soccer terminology a few years ago. Used by many, it is understood by few. My definition is "activities to improve vision, players' alertness and their speed of decision making." Activities that I favor tend to include multiple balls to stimulate the senses and create a demanding, high intensity training environment, taxing the player physically, technically and psychologically.

Here is a selection of small-sided games and activities to help enhance the quality of play from our players. This embodies the very performance of our basic techniques, whilst improving our technical ability, decision-making, and speed of play.

Speed of Play 1
Team

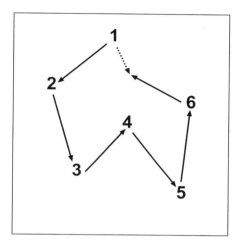

ORGANIZATION
- 30 x 45 yds
- 6 players numbered 1-6.
- One ball.

OBJECTIVE
- To lay down the fundamentals by creating good habits within the structure of sequential passing.
- Sequential passing = Player 1 passes to player 2, player 2 passes to player 3, etc.

COACHING POINTS
Technical
1. Instep pass.
2. Weight of pass.
3. Position of your body. Whenever possible, your body should be open to the field when receiving the ball. This will improve your vision and decision-making.
4. If receiving a pass, what foot do you receive it on?
   a.   If you receive a pass with the foot nearest the server, you will more than likely be facing that direction.
   b.   If you receive a pass with the foot furthest away from the

server, you will more than likely have opened up your body to allow the ball to run across the front of you. This will mean that your body is open to the field, so now you can see all of the field and not just one direction.

Tactical

1. Play the way you are facing.
2. Communication with or without the ball.
3. When to receive on the front or the back foot.
4. When to move to receive pass in open space

VARIATION

1. Increase the number of balls to two or have player 1 start with a ball and player 3 start with a ball. This will increase the speed of play and decision-making.
2. Keeping the ball up in the air and allowing one bounce. This improves control.

Speed of Play 2
Teams

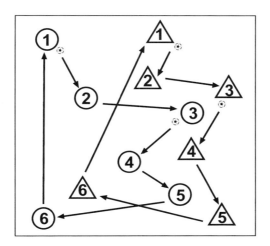

ORGANIZATION
- 30 x 45 yds
- 12 players, , split into 2 teams, one red, one blue, number them 1-6 on each team
- Two balls per team.

OBJECTIVE
To create vision and communication between players, to improve decision-making and speed of play, staying within the structure of sequential passing.

COACHING POINTS
Technical
1. Pass can now be given with the inside and outside of the foot.
2. Correct weight of pass.
3. Position of body when receiving pass.
4. Two touch.
Tactical
1. Play the way you are facing.
2. When to release pass.
3. What foot to receive pass on.
4. When to move into space to receive pass.

5. Decision-making should be done more quickly now.

VARIATION
- Use up to 4 soccer balls.
- Number players 1-12.
- Have 1, 3, 6 and 9 start with a ball and play in sequence.

Speed of Play 3

Teams

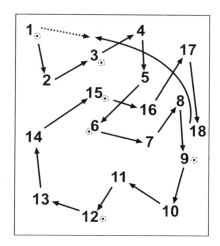

ORGANIZATION

- 30 x 45 yds
- 18 players, , split into 3 teams, one white, one red, one blue, number them 1-6 on each team.

OBJECTIVE

- To enhance vision and communication as well as to develop awareness and recognize a better understanding of space.
- To improve decision making and speed of play while staying within the structure of sequential passing.

COACHING POINTS

Technical

1. Pass can be given with the inside or outside of the foot.
2. Correct weight of pass.
3. Position of body when receiving pass.
4. Two touch.

Tactical

1. Play the way you are facing.
2. When to release pass.
3. What type of pass, inside or outside of foot.
4. Full use of space.

5. When and where to move into space to receive pass.
6. Decision making should be at its quickest.

VARIATION
- Use up to 6 balls.
- Number players 1-18.
- Have 1, 3, 6, 9, 12 and 15 start with a ball and play in sequence.

Speed of Play 4
2 Teams + Wall Players

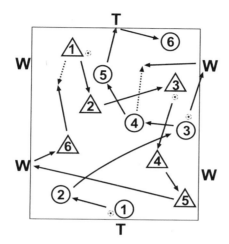

ORGANIZATION
- 30 x 45 yds
- 18 players split into 3 teams, numbered 1-6
- Two teams inside the grid wearing different colors
- Each team has 2 balls
- The other team is on the outside of the grid, four wall players, two each side and half of the grid and the other are targets on either end of the grid.

OBJECTIVE
- To develop a better understanding of how and when to use various techniques such as: 1-2's, takeovers, overlaps, wall passes, penetrating passes and supporting runs.
- We still stay with the sequential passing, which will not include playing a pass off a wall player.
- For instance, player 1 will pass to a wall player or target player, player 2 now needs to be the player receiving it. This will help in the decision making and speed of play.

COACHING POINTS
Technical
1. Pass can be given by the inside or outside of the foot.
2. Correct weight of pass.
3. Position of your body when receiving.
4. Head up.

Tactical
1. Play the way you are facing.
2. When to use wall/target players.
3. When receiving pass from wall player, body should be open to the field and pass should be received on back foot.
4. When to release pass.
5. You should be aware of what is going on around you.

VARIATION
- Unlimited touches on the ball.
- Every third pass has to go long.

Speed of Play 5
Playmaker

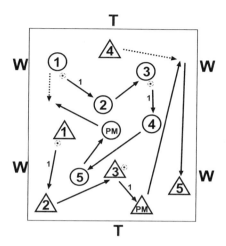

ORGANIZATION
- 30 x 45 yds
- 18 players split into 3 teams
- Oneteam consists of 4 wall players, 2 on each side of the grid and 2 targets, 1 at each end,
- The other 2 teams consist of 5 players numbered 1-5 and a playmaker,
- Each team inside the grid has 2 balls.

OBJECTIVE
- To make the playmaker create a rhythm of play as well as dictate the style and speed of play.
- We can facilitate this by requiring that every third pass be played by the playmaker.
- The playmaker starts with his first pass to player 1 and player 3 starts with his first pass to player 4.
- If you use a wall or target player now, it counts as a pass and you must still play it in sequence.

COACHING POINTS
Technical
1. Correctly weighted pass.
2. Good first touch.
3. Position of body when receiving pass.
4. Head up.
Tactical
1. Timing of pass by the playmaker.
2. Decision making by the playmaker - is it correct?
3. Communication of the playmaker.
4. Does he dictate the rhythm of play?

VARIATION
- Go with 4 field players numbered 1-4, 1 playmaker and 1 supporting player.
- Supporting player now has to receive every other pass from the playmaker.
- For example, playmaker to wall player to supporting player, or playmaker to next number to supporting player.

Speed of Play 6
6 v 3 Possession

40 X 40 yds

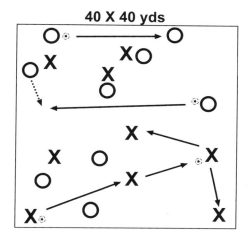

ORGANIZATION
- 40 x 40 yds divided into 2 halves
- 18 players split into 2 teams of 9, one team in each half
- You should have 6v3 on each side of the field and the 6 should be in possession of 2 balls.

OBJECTIVE
- To play 6v3 possession soccer, two touch, in a tight area where you are being pressured and have to maintain a high level of awareness of what is going on around you, as the other team is performing the same exercise.
- The 3 players who are defending now have 2 balls to try to win back.

COACHING POINTS
Technical
1. Correctly weighted passes.
2. Good first touch.
3. Position of body when receiving pass.
4. Head up.
Tactical
1. Timing.

2. Weight of pass.
3. Good decision making by player in possession of ball.
4. Good team communication.
5. Good team support.
6. Good use of space.

Playing in the Defensive Third 1
Playing Out of the Back

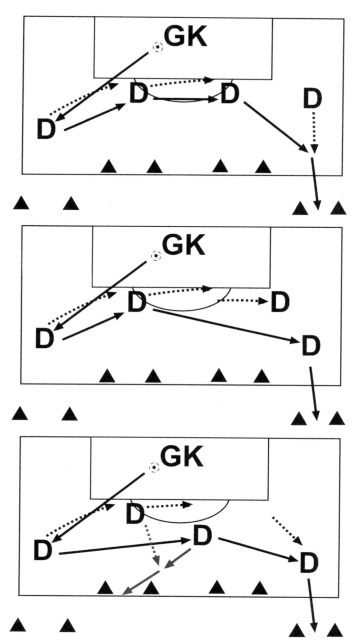

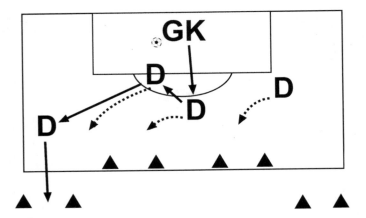

ORGANIZATION
- Half the field
- 4 defenders and GK
- 8 cones
- Supply of balls

OBJECTIVE
To develop passing patterns for the defenders so they are all on the same page. When playing the ball out of the back, use the goals as targets.

COACHING POINTS
- When receiving a pass, look to receive the ball on your far foot so your body opens up in the direction you want to pass to.
- Develop an understanding of rhythm, balance and movement between defenders
- Helping the defenders keep possession of the ball and to be creative in starting an attack
- First touch into space and then deliver
- Limit the touches on the ball
- Defenders should squeeze the space behind the defender in possession
- Move the ball quickly between the defenders to transition quickly up the field

Playing in the Defensive Third 2
Functional Training of the Back Four

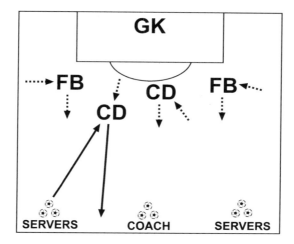

ORGANIZATION
- On half the field
- 2 center backs, 2 fullbacks and 1 goalkeeper
- 2-4 servers on each flank
- Coach in the center area with several balls.

OBJECTIVE
- Train the back four on how to step up and move together and when and who drops off.
- To develop balance and rhythm.
- The technical application of clearing the ball.

ACTION
- Servers or coach play ball into the middle of defense.
- Coach looks for the co-ordination of movement between the back four to cover the space behind the player stepping up to attack the ball.

COACHING POINTS
- Communication between the back four and the goalkeeper.
- Balance between the defenders covering the space behind the player attacking the ball.
- The back four stepping up behind the ball after it has been cleared.

Playing in the Defensive Third 3
Functional Training of the Two Center Backs

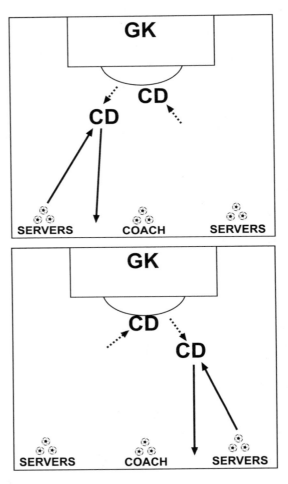

ORGANIZATION
● On half the field
● 2 center backs & 1goalkeeper,
● 2-4 servers on each flank, the coach in the central area with several balls.

OBJECTIVE
● Tactically train the two center backs to work in tandem.

- Who steps up and who drops off?
- The technical application of clearing the ball with one touch.

ACTION

- On the coach's signal the server plays the ball into the middle of defense.
- The ball side central defender steps up and attacks the ball.
- The weak side center defender covers him by dropping off between the central defender and the goalkeeper.
- When the ball has been cleared, both players step up.

COACHING POINTS

- Communication between the goalkeeper and the two center backs.
- When to step and when to drop off.
- The technical application of clearing the ball.

Playing in the Defensive Third 4
Step and Squeeze

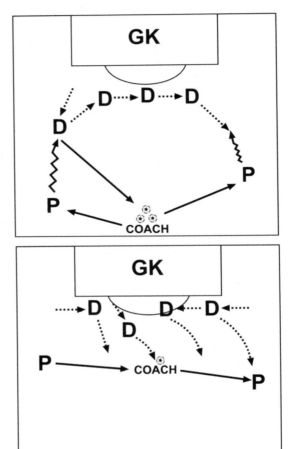

ORGANIZATION
- Half the field
- 4 defenders and a goalkeeper
- Two wide players
- The coach in central areas
- Supply of balls.

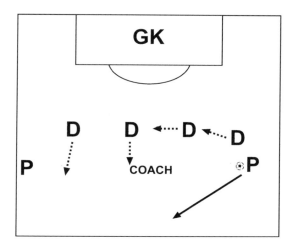

OBJECTIVE

For the back 4 to move together with the closest defender step-ping up to press the ball while the other defenders squeeze the space and cover behind.

COACHING POINTS

- Communication between the back four and the goalkeeper.
- Rhythm and balance in the movements of the back four.
- Stepping up behind the ball.
- When attacker drives at the defenders, the defenders retreat to a predetermined point and hold their line.
- This we refer to as the point of confrontation.

APPLICATION

- Players move forward and play the ball back to the coach or opposite player.
- We are looking to develop movement between the defenders and an understanding of when to drop and when to step up.

Playing in the Defensive Third 5
Defending

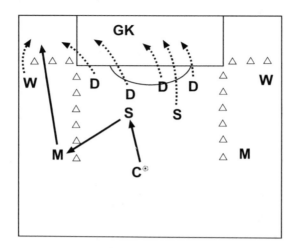

ORGANIZATION
- Area marked off with cones, 16 yard line to touch line, 10 yards outside the 18 yard box, half of the field.
- 4 defenders, 6 attacking players, server (coach)
- Supply of balls

OBJECTIVE
- To teach the individual players within the back four their responsibilities when the ball is played behind, in front and wide of them
- Also, when to step up, drop off and press.

COACHING POINTS
- 1st defender (closest defender) gets pressure on the ball.
- Deny penetration
- Decide direction to send winger
- Balance and movement of other defenders in relation to the ball and attackers
- Distance between defenders
- Do they zone or mark up?
- Organization of goalkeeper,
- Communication,

- When to step up when the ball is played back to the midfield player at edge of the box.

ACTION
- Coach plays the ball into the striker.
- Striker plays to defensive midfielder.
- Defensive midfielder plays ball behind the cones for the winger to cross.
- Progress to winger passing the ball back to center midfielder.

Playing in the Defensive Third 6
Defensive Cover Through Movement and Communication

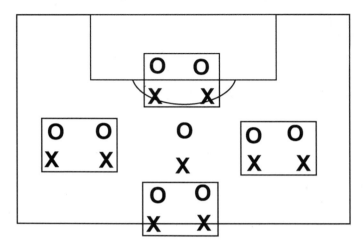

ORGANIZATION
- 4 x 20 x 15 yd grids spread out in half the field
- 2 v 2 in each grid, 1 free defender from each team outside the grids
- Supply of balls

OBJECTIVE
- Each pair tries to keep possession and combine to dribble the ball over the opposition's line
- Opposition must defend their line while trying to score on the other team
- The two free defenders add additional support when needed, but can go into a grid only when called by their teammates in that grid
- A team can only call for support when defending and the free defender must leave the grid when they have won possession

COACHING POINTS
- Position of the first defender
- Position of support of second defender in relation to the ball and the attackers

Playing out of the Midfield 1
Training the Two Center Midfielders

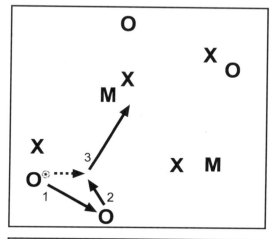

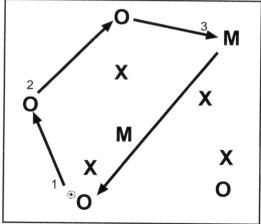

ORGANIZATION
- 25-40 yd sqare in the center of the field
- 4 v 4 + 2, the plus 2 are the two center mids
- Supply of balls

OBJECTIVE
To train the two center mids to combine with each other at the right time, creating options for the team in possession

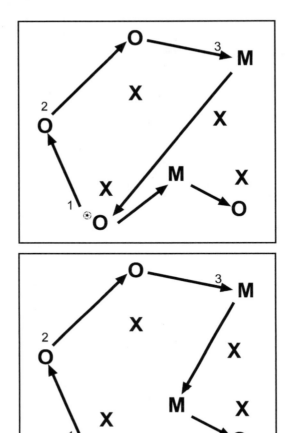

COACHING POINTS
● Keeping the touches to a minimum under pressure
● Playing with heads up to improve vision
● Keeping posssession of the ball

VARIATIONS
1. 4 v 4 + 2 - team in possession must make every 3rd pass to a center midfield player
2. 4 v 4 + 2 - team in possession must make every 3rd pass to a center midfield player whose next pass must be long
3. Same, but as the center mid plays it long, the other center mid must receive it short from the receiver

4. Same, but now when the center mid receives it, he must now find the other center mid, so the other center mid's timing of the run and angle of the run are very important

Playing out of the Midfield 2
Training the Flank Players

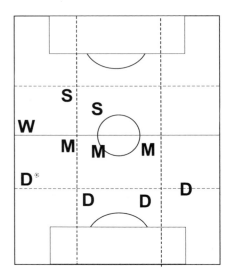

ORGANIZATION
- Divide the field into thirds both ways
- Supply of balls
- Work only on the flanks on both sides
- Create a numbers up scenario 4 v 3
- Coach or player can act as server to begin the activity.

OBJECTIVE
- This is functional as well as economical.
- It takes part in the are of the field that is relevant to the players operating there.
- Emphasis will be on combination play to release the winger

COACHING POINTS
- Movement of the winger relevant to the visual cues from the player in possession of the ball (defender).
- Angle of runs.
- Disguise of runs.
- Angle of passing.

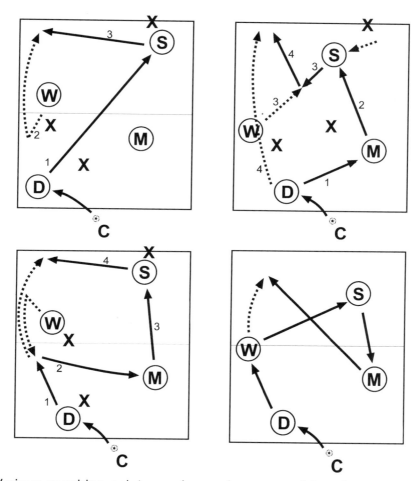

Various coaching points can be made on any of the players in this activity. What is important is that the group maintains possession, while probing until the moment presents itself to penetrate either with or without the ball. Begin with the opposition being passive. Increase pressure steadily until you are at match conditions. Work with groups on both sides at a time.

Playing out of the Midfield 3
Quick Transitional Counter Attacking Play

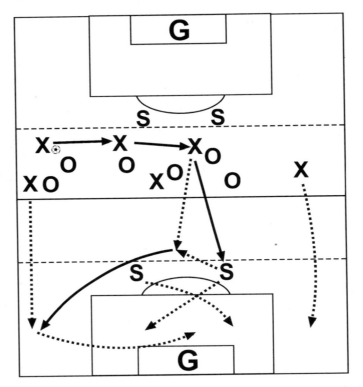

ORGANIZATION
● Full field divided into thirds
● 18 players and 2 goalkeepers, 4 strikers, 2 on each side of the field in their own attacking thirds, 1 defender each side picking up the 2 attackers, 6 players from each team play between the edge of the attacking third and the half way line, 1 team defends and the other attacks.
● Supply of balls.

OBJECTIVE
● Coach starts by directing play.
● The objective is to keep possession of the ball until an opening creates the opportunity to play the ball forward to one of the two strikers.

• Then support the strikers at pace from behind, getting numbers forward and creating scoring opportunities.

COACHING POINTS
• Combination play between the midfielders to create passing opportunities
• To penetrate with support to the strikers
• Third man running
• Overlapping runs in support
• Penetrating runs
• Movement of strikers
• Angle of runs

PROGRESSION
Add in 2 additional defenders to mark up both strikers on both sides, and now this activity becomes realistic, as pressure is added to the strikers.

Playing out of the Midfield 4

Counter Attacking Against a Pressing Team

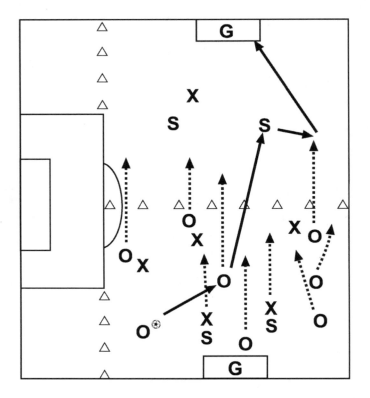

ORGANIZATION

- Full field divided into thirds
- 18 players and 2 goalkeepers, 4 strikers, 2 on each side of the field in their own attacking thirds, 1 defender each side picking up the 2 attackers, 6 players from each team play between the edge of the attacking third and the half way line, 1 team defends and the other attacks.
- Supply of balls.

OBJECTIVE
- Coach starts by directing play.
- The objective is to keep possession of the ball until an opening creates the opportunity to play the ball forward to one of the two strikers.
- Then support the strikers at pace from behind, getting numbers forward and creating scoring opportunities.

COACHING POINTS
- Combination play between the midfielders to create passing opportunities
- To penetrate with support to the strikers
- Third man running
- Overlapping runs in support
- Penetrating runs
- Movement of strikers
- Angle of runs

PROGRESSION
Add in 2 additional defenders to mark up both strikers on both sides, and now this activity becomes realistic, as pressure is added to the strikers.

Playing out of the Midfield 5
Playing Against Pressure

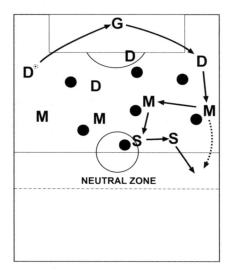 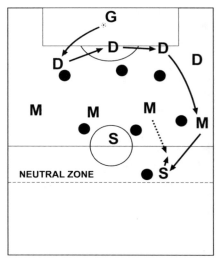

ORGANIZATION
- 11 v 7,
- Supply of balls,
- Set of pinnies, 10 blues, 7 reds.

OBJECTIVE
- Training players to move the ball quickly out of the defensive half (neutral zone).
- Playing against pressure from the 7 pressing players.

COACHING POINTS
- Limit touches.
- Combining to enter into neutral zone.
- Players can only receive the ball in the neutral zone if they are running into it and not in there waiting to receive the pass.

PROGRESSION

- One striker steps into the neutral zone and is man marked.
- Now we have 10 v 6 in defensive half.
- When it is on, you can play directly to the high striker, but we can only score by the third man running.

OBJECTIVE

Goalkeeper starts play by distributing to an open player.
From there, the team in possession works hard to play quickly in order to transition forward quickly, before the pressing team has time to get organized.

Playing out of the Midfield 6
Playing Against a Square Defense

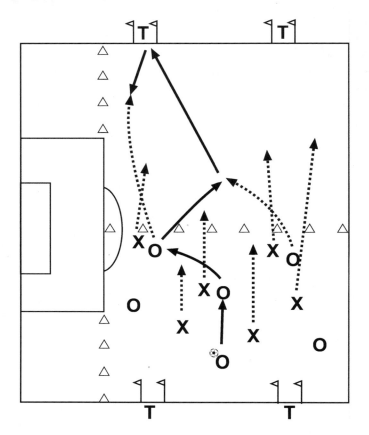

ORGANIZATION
- Run a line of cones level with the 18 yard box to the touch line and divide the field in two with a line of cones up the center
- 16 players divided into 2 teams of 6 and 4 targets,
- The target players play within 2 goals on either side of the field, each goal is 5 yards wide.

OBJECTIVE

- Both teams are playing against an offside trap.
- In this case, this is the center line, not the opposition.
- Both teams have to press the ball in the opponent's half of the field.
- When they have been successful and won the ball, they must bring the ball back into their own half and penetrate back into their opponent's half, staying onside.
- Once inside their opponent's half, they must play into the targets and the target must complete the move by playing back to him or a member of that team.
- If they lose possession to the opposition, the opposition can counter going into their targets again, playing against an offside trap.
- You cannot win the ball in your opponent's half and go straight to target players.
- You must bring the ball back into your own half and build up the attack from there.

COACHING POINTS

- Playing against an offside trap.
- All players must be in one half, either pressing or attacking.
- Players should be looking for ways to beat the trap while keeping pressure on.
- A ball played from in to out.
- A ball played from out to in.
- A long ball played over the top.
- Combination play.
- Overlapping runs.
- Bending runs.
- Player takes it on the dribble.

Playing in the Final Third 1
Posting Up Finishing Activities

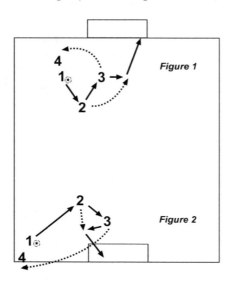

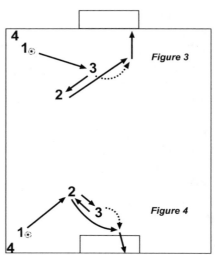

ORGANIZATION
- 60 x 40 yds
- 16 players, 2 goalkeepers,
- 2 full size goals
- Supply of balls.

OBJECTIVE
To create a repetitive activity where a player can work on various methods of striking the ball to goal.

COACHING POINTS
- Pace of the pass into the server.
- First touch of the server and quality of pass to player posting up.
- Quality of strike from the player shooting.

Figure 1
Short pass, 5 yards.
Player 1 passes to player 2.
Player 2 passes to player 3.
Player 3 lays it to player 2 to shoot inside.
Player 3 rotates to player 4.
Player 2 now posts up.

Figure 2
Longer pass, 25 yards.

Figure 3
Player 1 passes to player 3.
Player 3 sets it for player 2 and peels out, keeping body open to goal.
Player 2 threads the ball through to player 3 to continue with a good strike on goal

Figure 4
Player 1 passes to player 2.
Player 2 passes to player 3.
Player 3 passes it back to player 2 and player 3 peels off for player 2 to play it in for player 3 to finish.

Playing in the Final Third 2
Twin Striker Play

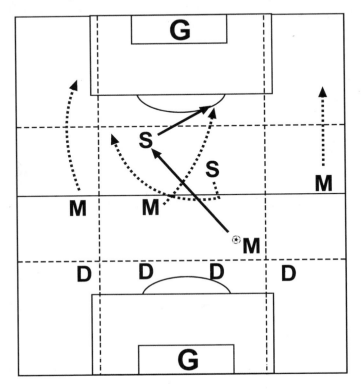

ORGANIZATION
- 25 x 40 yds
- 4 players, 2 central midfielders, 2 strikers
- Supply of balls.

OBJECTIVE
To recreate passing options to the strikers from the supporting and attacking midfielders.

COACHING POINTS
- Far striker maintains depth at an angle to the near striker.
- The near striker drives towards the midfielder in possession of the ball, as though looking for the pass.

- The midfielder bypasses the near striker and plays to the far striker as the near striker peels inside across the face of the far striker.
- By doing so, the near striker creates space by taking the defender with him, and as the defender follows the supporting midfielder he makes a penetrating run into the space vacated, giving the far striker the option of playing a good penetrating pass in behind for the midfielder to go through on.
- Convincing decoy run by near striker.
- Pace of pass from midfielder.
- Angle of pass into striker from midfielder.
- Good quality lay off from far striker.

Playing in the Final Third 3
Overlapping Into the Final Third

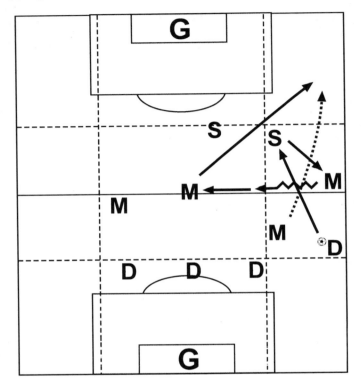

ORGANIZATION
- 25 x 40 yds
- 4 players, 2 midfielders, 1 striker, 1 defender
- Supply of balls.

OBJECTIVE
To recreate the situation where the players can identify at what moment to overlap, through verbal and visual cues.

PATTERN
- Defender drops his head to deliver the ball to the striker.
- Striker receives and plays wide to the supporting wide midfielder.
- Wide player begins to bring the ball inside to the center of the field, creating space on the flank.

• The center midfielder bends his run towards the flank.

COACHING POINTS
• Eye contact between players prior to pass.
• The wide player driving inwards towards center to create space and also provide a visual cue for the center midfielder to read.
• Pace of pass from defender.
• Angle of run from striker.
• Timing of run of center midfielder to overlap.
• Angle of pass from winger to overlapping player.

Playing in the Final Third 4
Cross Over Runs in Attack

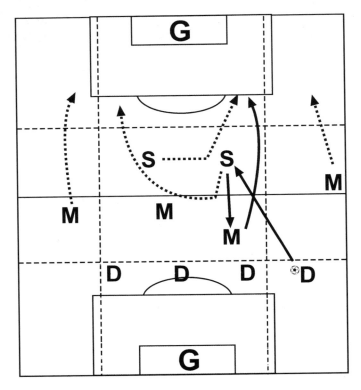

ORGANIZATION
- 25 x 40 yds
- 4 players, 1 defender, 1 midfielder, 2 strikers
- Supply of balls.

OBJECTIVE
To recreate passing options to the strikers in the middle to attacking third of the field when playing out of the defensive third.

COACHING POINTS
- Defender plays a good weighted pass into the nearest striker.
- First striker controls it and lays it back to the supporting center midfielder.
- The first striker who just laid the ball off starts his run towards the center midfielder in possession of the ball.

- After 2-3 yards, he peels off inside, but has to create space in behind himself.
- The second striker now begins his run, beginning flat towards where the first striker was.
- Then, as the center midfielder in possession of the ball plays a penetrating pass in behind the first striker, the second striker matches his run to the flight of the ball.
- Pace of the pass from the defender.
- Angle of the run from the second striker who must stay on-side.
- Timing of the pass from the center midfielder.
- Timing of the run from the second striker.
- Creation of space with the run of the first striker.

Playing in the Final Third 5
Across the Face Runs

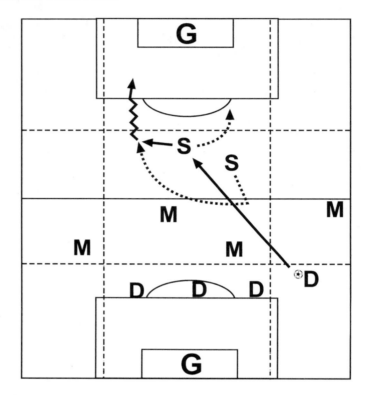

ORGANIZATION
- 25 x 40 yds
- 4 players, 1 defender, 1 midfielder and 2 strikers
- Supply of balls

OBJECTIVE
To recreate passing options to the strikers in the middle to attacking third of the field when playing out of the defensive third.
COACHING POINTS
- The near striker drives towards the defender in possession of the ball.
- The defender drops his head and plays a good weighted pass into the near striker.
- The near striker peels away towards the center of the field,

across the face of the far striker, who is directly behind the near striker.

- As the ball arrives at the far striker, the near striker is now in a position to receive the ball from the far striker who is looking to lay the ball off to the near striker, then turn himself and follow up in support of the shot or rebound.
- Timing of the run of near striker.
- Pace of the pass from defender.
- Angle of pass from defender.
- Quality of lay from far striker.

Playing in the Final Third 6
Decoy Runs in Attack

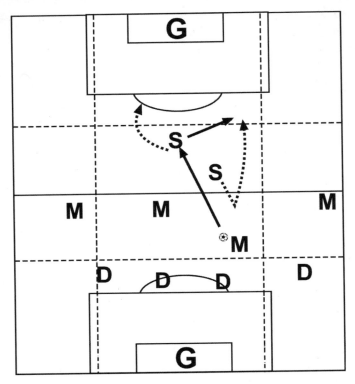

ORGANIZATION
- 25 x 40 yard area
- 4 players, 2 central midfielders & 2 strikers
- Supply of balls

OBJECTIVE
- To recreate passing options to the strikers in the middle to attacking third of the field
- Playing through midfield.

COACHING POINTS
- The near striker drives towards the center and calls for the ball from the midfielder in possession.
- As the center midfielder looks to play it in to him, the near

striker peels out, creating a passing option and passing seam to play to the far striker who is at an angle behind the near striker.

- The midfielder plays a good weighted pass into the far striker by passing the near striker.
- This enables the near striker to be facing the far striker who now has the choice of holding it and turning on his own or laying it into the path of the near striker to go to goal or shoot.
- Convincing decoy run from the near striker.
- Pace of pass from midfielder.
- Angle of pass from midfielder.
- Decision to hold it & turn or lay it off for near striker from far striker.

Playing in the Final Third 7
Functional Shooting Activities

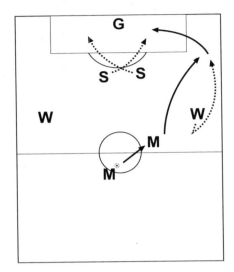 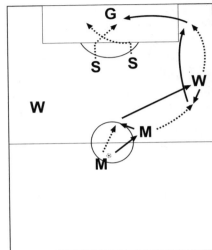

ORGANIZATION
- All the members of the squad involved in the relevant areas of the field that applies to them
- Number of balls
- Two corner flags placed 5 yards in from the touch line, level with the 18 yard box.

OBJECTIVE
- To create repetitions relevant to the players operating in that area of the field.
- Also to work within the limitation of the patterns of play that replicate the game situation.

COACHING POINTS
- Quality of the first touch.
- Quality of the pass.
- Pace of the pass, when to drive it and when to float it.
- Timing of the runs from the wing players, angles of their runs, shape of the flank player's body type to cross driven near or whipped in far post.

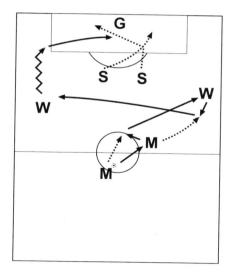

- Timing of the runs from strikers. Does the first attacker get across the body of the goalkeeper? Does the 2nd attacker open up his body as he follows the ball and finally, do we get a quality strike on goal?

These activities can be very effective, visually, on a team as it reinforces the team philosophy and play. In this case, playing it wide through combination play and allowing the striker numerous opportunities to get quality strikes on goal.

Playing in the Final Third 8

Shooting Rotation Activities

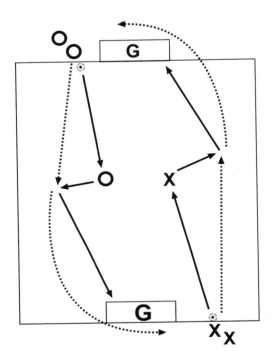

ORGANIZATION

- 30 x 40 yds
- Two full size goals on each end
- The squad, 2 players as targets inside the grid.
- Supply of balls

OBJECTIVE

To create quick fire and numerous shooting opportunities for all the members of the squad in a simple rotation.

COACHING POINTS

- All technical applications when striking the ball.
- Vary the angle and service to the shooter.
- Hit the target

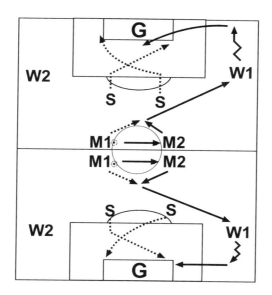

ORGANIZATION
- Full field, field split into 2 halves,
- 18 players, 2 wingers, 4 strikers, 2 midfielders, 1 goalkeeper on each half
- Supply of balls

OBJECTIVE
To create game-like situation without pressure in a repetitious form to perfect quality of technique.

COACHING POINTS
- Quality of pass
- Quality of cross
- Timing of runs
- Variation of finishing, heading, volley, half volley, set ups, etc.
- Vocal and visual cues recognized.

ACTION
- M1 plays M2 to set it.
- M1 plays to W1 who takes a touch for S1 & S2 to go near and far post for a cross.

Playing in the Final Third 9
Box on Box Shooting

ORGANIZATION
- Two 18 yard boxes
- 4 v 4 + 2 goalkeepers on each half, 4 reds, 4 blues.
- Supply of balls

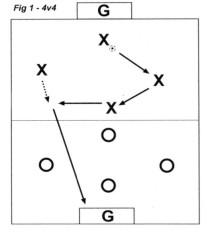

Fig 1 - 4v4

OBJECTIVE
To create long distance shooting opportunities from different angles from outside the 18 yard box.

COACHING POINTS
- Position of body when the player shoots.
- When to go for power over accuracy.
- Technical application of the actual shot.
- Emphasis on hitting the target.

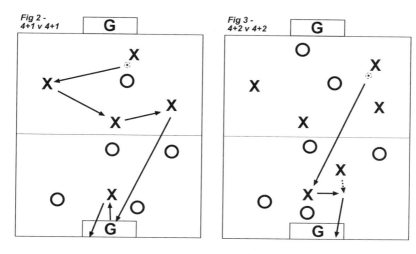

VARIATION & PROGRESSION

Figure 2: Add a striker inside the box for any knock downs from the keeper.

Figure 3: Add 2 strikers inside the box to put the 4 players under pressure to get their shot off.

Also, they can be used to combine with to create opportunities from different angles. Remember, the shots must come from outside the 18 yard mark.

Playing in the Final Third 10
Near and Far Post Finishing Activity

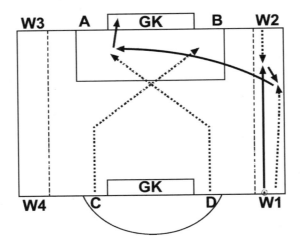

ORGANIZATION
- 18 yard box with two full size goals facing each other and two
- 5 yard channels on the outside edges (see diagram)
- All team members
- Supply of balls
- Four wingers on each corner with the rest of the players spread out evenly on the outside of the posts.

OBJECTIVE
To create numerous quality services into dangerous areas from wingers, for the attackers to finish with a quality strike on goal.

COACHING POINTS
- W1 plays a well paced pass into W2.
- W2 comes short and sets the pass up for W1 to whip a good pass into the goal.
- As W1 makes his first pass, strikers C & D are making forward runs until W2 sets the ball.
- At that time C & D switch: D going far post, C going near post.
- After the finish on goal, W1 & W2 go back to their original starting points and the opposite side repeats the process for A & B to go.

- Pace of the pass from W1.
- First touch of W2.
- Cross: driven, lofted, swerved into goal or away (quality).
- Timing of the strikers' runs.
- Communication from strikers.
- Change of pace and direction from strikers on switch
- W3, W4, A and B perform the same exercise on the opposite side.